Magical Hearth

Magical Hearth

Home for the Modern Pagan

Janet Thompson

SAMUEL WEISER, INC.

York Beach, Maine

First published in 1995 by
Samuel Weiser, Inc.
P. O. Box 612
York Beach, ME 03910–0612

02 01 00 99 98 97 96 95
10 9 8 7 6 5 4 3 2 1

Library of Congress Cataloging-in-Publication Data
Thompson, Janet.
    Magical hearth : home for the modern pagan / Janet Thompson.
       p.   cm.
    Includes index.
    1. Witchcraft.   2. Herbs—Miscellanea.   3. Paganism—Rituals.
    4. Rites and ceremonies.   5. Magic.   I. Title.
    BF1566.T464 1995
    133.4'3—dc20   95–17611
                                                    CIP
ISBN 0-87728-824-0
CCP

Cover illustration Copyright © 1995 Catherine Rose Crowther

Typeset in 11 point Times New Roman

Printed in the United States of America

The paper used in this publication meets the minimum requirements of the American National Standard for Permanence of Paper for Printed Library Materials Z39.48-1984.

Table of Contents

For my daughter Hannah,
who made her journey to me
during this book's creation.

Acknowledgments

I have been blessed in my life with so many who love me and encourage my work. Friends and family are precious. I want to convey my love and appreciation, but sometimes words are not adequate to the task.

To Kelly, who's love and laughter enriches my life daily; and Aileen, who's losses have been great but who still had the words to keep me focused; and Andrea, for our shared memories; and Dad, for being proud of me when I was not proud of myself; and Gary, for encouragement beyond the call.

Dina and Ian, with your thirty-something laughter and your love. I cannot express what you mean to me. With the soul of a pagan you have lifted my spirits at times when no other would do. I love you.

Dave and Gisele, you have given me a lifetime of love already. Your encouragement and strength are a foundation for so much I have learned. The road less traveled is truly a path worth walking.

Karen, you will never know what our friendship has meant to me. I can only hope you have some idea of how strongly you touch my heart. You give me a kick when I need one and a chuckle when I don't. May our morning ritual go on for a long, long time.

To Jim—hey, Bandit.
To Robin—a fine woman and witch.

And to my mother, Marian, who cannot read these words but who knows how much I love her.

May you all have love and joy, for each of you gives in abundance.

Introduction

Heating, cooking, and light have been necessary elements of life since the dawn of reasoning in humankind. From earliest civilization to present day life, the hearth (or kitchen) in the home is a central focus.

In ancient Rome, Vesta was Goddess of the hearth. It was a great honor for one's daughter to join the order of the Vestal Virgins, who's main function was to tend the city hearth or central fire. These women were highly regarded and treated with reverence. After many years of service, they were free to leave the order. But it was considered a great privilege to serve.

In Roman households, the family gathered together each day to pay homage to Vesta and a sacrifice was made to Her at the family hearth. Each household, in Rome and in many other ancient cultures, had its individual altars at which to worship. The sacrifice (usually as simple as salt and flour, esentials in a home) represented thanks. On very special feast or celebratory days, the sacrifice was enhanced accordingly.

Hearth-fires throughout history have been regarded as the hub of life. From the hearth comes heat to cook food and shape metal, teas to heal, warmth for the cold winters (often the entire family slept around the hearth) and light. In castles of old, the Great Hall had one or more hearths. Visitors and family usually slept in the hall and servants kept the fires going. All gatherings began here; feasts were served beside these fires.

The hearth functions in history as a magical necessity, for the Delphic oracles threw sacred and potent herbs into the brazier to enable them to see the prophecies. Different herbs may have been hallucinogens or narcotics which (when inhaled) would alter the state of conscious awareness.

The ancient Celts believed that homefires must be lit only once a year. On the eve of Samhain (modern-day Halloween), the Celtic New Year, the old fire was allowed to go out and a new one lit. The earliest riser in the household would rekindle the morning fire with a still-burning ember from the communal feast fire of the previous night. Thus the hearth remained continuous until the next Samhain. The Celts also believed that ancestral stories of bravery and magic should be told at the family hearth. The hearth lay as a witness to history.

Since the advent of central heating and the stove, the meaning of the hearth has changed. Today, the hearth is the home. Home is a private place; a place where we can be ourselves, watch our children grow, entertain our friends, and feel our magic. Many people go through the motions of magic and power on the path to inner growth and enlightenment without really reaping the benefits. If you wish to invite magic into your life, you must first invite magic into your home. You must create a place where magic can flourish; where it can become a part of you, for your home is a part of you.

Each room can become the source from which different types of magic flow. Your home should be as comfortable as possible for you and your inner work. It is the base for all the magical functions in your life. You may create magical outlets elsewhere, but the roots of your magic start at home. You relax at home, you meditate at home, and you prepare for whatever magic you will be doing at home. Your home must reflect your spiritual self in order that you may prepare your physical and psychic self for magical service.

This book is designed for people who use the elements in their spiritual lives; for those who need be in touch with the powers around them. Shamanism, Neo-Paganism, Wicca (and all religions which deal with inner strength, outer love, and healing) need sanctuaries where solo or group practitioners can become one with things magic. We must have a place for our work, our tools, our beliefs and our growth. This place must be created. Few of us are lucky enough to live in perfection. There can be drawbacks to any home one might have. Close neighbors, loud noises, less than adequate heat, or numerous other negatives can inhibit the frequency or intensity of magical work.

This is a book about how to permeate your home with— your magic, your forces, your Self. Open wide your doors and invite magic in.

1

Magical Hearth

or most people, the kitchen represents the old-fashioned idea of the hearth. The good aroma of cooking, the warmth of the gathered family, or the solitude of the kitchen table can provide comfort and peace. The kitchen can be the most hectic room in a house, as well.

Often, the smell of something baking stirs memories deep inside us. Apples and cinnamon, pies, stews, and steamy vegetables greet us as we come through the door. Aromas like these bring to us the scents of childhood. We can close our eyes and be back in our mother's or grandmother's kitchen again.

Magic in the kitchen happens whether the practitioner is aware of it or not. For instance, when you reach for a certain spice or herb with which to season a dish you are preparing, you will have a preconceived idea of what that herb will do to flavor the recipe. This positive expectation, in itself, is magic. You are actually able to visualize the dish when done, and you can taste it, too. This kind of pre-expectation is the groundwork for magical practice.

Many cooks use intuition when they create new dishes. This intuition is guided by two things—practical prior experience, and the force of the herb. Each herb has its own particular vibratory energy. When people, having worked with herbs before, are preparing a dish, often they will add an herb that they may not have used before. This experimentation is guided by the properties of the herb and how each would enhance the dish, not only culinarily, but magically. Consider, for a moment, the herb basil. One of the most common dishes that lovers prepare for each other is pasta. The most common ingredient in pasta dishes is basil. Basil has long been thought to increase and strengthen affairs of the heart. It has been used in love sachets and magic for a very long time. Instinctually, people will use basil when cooking for a lover, because they are unknowingly aware of the power of that herb.

Corn dollies have retained a place in many kitchens. The history of these dollies is rather interesting in that it presents one of the clearest examples of continuity in the ancient Celtic cultures. Corn dollies are traditionally made with the last corn from the harvest. This new corn dolly replaces last year's which is burned in the fires at either the Autumnal Equinox or Samhain. This burning of the dolly is to give thanks for the harvest. At the Celtic festival of Imolg (February 2nd) the dolly is dressed to play the role of "Biddy" for rituals of fertility for the growing season to come.

The kitchen is one place where the changing of the seasons is the most noticeable. Cooking smells shift with the time of year. In the spring we have fresh summer vegetables. Bar-B-Ques leave their very distinctive aromas in the summer air; watermelon, peaches, and tasty, seasonal fruits make their way to our tables. In the fall (my very favorite time) we have squash, sweet potatoes, corn, and all of the wonderful results of the harvest. In the winter, with the celebrations of Thanksgiving and Yuletide, we are tantalized with the smell of turkey, ham, nutmeg and pine. The smells of the seasons find a source in the kitchen.

I love the smells in my kitchen at harvest time. Not only do I like all the harvest vegetables, but the bunches of medicinal and magical herbs that hang drying in my kitchen leave their particular scent. They also add a touch of country in my city home. The deep purple flowers of the clover, the white of the yarrow, and the dusty green of the sage, all help to make my kitchen homey. The scent of lemon balm, sage, lavender, peppermint, and bay berry drift in the air.

When cooking or preparing medicinal or magical recipes and teas, we are practicing hearth magic. We stir, we taste, we add a pinch of this, and a dash of that. This is magic. It imbibes the creation with love, energy and intensity. It does not matter that the people creating are aware of this or not. The magic is still being generated. Power is released from us to the thing we are constructing. This power will then increase the potentiality of the brew. Thus, the dish will be tastier, the tea will heal more rapidly and the incense/pot-pourri/oil will be stronger magically. This is hearth magic, and people who put a part of themselves into what is being done are practitioners of hearth magic.

Often if I am cooking a meal, I will put the required herb into the dish and then I will take an added pinch and burn it on the stove or over an incense coal. If, for example, I am in need of a sound sleep that night, I will burn a pinch of peppermint and cinquefoil. The magical properties of peppermint include sleep aid and cinquefoil will generate psychic and prophetic dreams. Each has its own power. If I need to touch with Spirit, I burn willow leaves. If I—or anyone I know—is having financial difficulty, I will burn patchouli or bergamot. I am already in the kitchen cooking, so I make use of the moment to connect magically.

The kitchen is a magical hearth for many people, and they use the room in different ways. A number of people I know often light candles when making something particularly important. The flame of the candle provides warmth of atmosphere, purification of air, and a representation of the fire element. Burning herbs for their different properties is a way to utilize the earth and fire elements together.

Cauldrons, brooms, salt, and herbal teas all have a place in the kitchen. Each of these items is so ordinary that they could not possibly look out of place. Cauldrons are any pan or pot used to heat something made with care and love. From the stew pot to the Sabbat fire-pot. Each is a representation of the Goddess. She answers to many names; perhaps her most famous persona is that of Cerridwen, Cerridwen, being a celtic Goddess who has great strength of character. Her courage might only be tested by her quick temper. This Lady is an embodiment of all that is woman. That is not to say that all women are the characteristic match to Cerridwen. On the contrary, there are as many types of personalities and traits as there are Gods and Goddesses to represent them. Cerridwen is the seer of prophecies; the teller of stories; she is the caregiver and healer.

The broom, as any Wiccan could tell you, is the wand incognito. It was used in many traditions to ride and jump the crops to ensure good harvests. It also presented a boundary to a newly wed couple. This couple could envision the land of love and family beyond the broom. When they jumped over to the other side, they now moved as a connected pair. The broom has always swept the negative away. Doorsteps must be swept regularly to banish negativity as it tries to cross the threshold.

Salt is one of the strongest representations of the earth element. Rice, dirt, stones, herbs, vegetables, and fruits can all be a part of that representation. But salt remains one of the most versatile. It is used to cleanse any magical tool, and is an ingredient in prosperity and protective work. Its most fascinating trait is that no matter how small it breaks, its form remains the same; that is, a perfect cube. The cube, like other symbols (pentagram, circle, etc.) is continuous. There is no beginning and end. This is representative of not only the earth and earth elementals, but of the Grand Plan.

Kitchen Magic

In doing any magical work or ritualization, the most important ingredient is, of course, intent. Do magical work only with good intent. It stands to reason that if we do good we will receive in kind. If our intentions are negative, this, too, will result in a like return. Your work must always be done knowing that it harms no one including you.

Ritual is carried out throughout our day. We do not have to be conscious of this fact, but none-the-less, it goes on day in and day out. Aside from the spiritual rituals of our beliefs (no matter the faith or path), we conduct rituals of cleansing ourselves, i.e., baths, washing hands, brushing hair and teeth, etc. Anything which is done repeatedly and in the same manner to achieve the same end is ritual. We expect the end results and are visualizing them thus. In this manner, everyday motions and behavior become ritualized. But the very best kind of ritual is one of which we are aware. The more we imbibe the work with our power, the greater the reward. As with any task, effort is the key. This is not to say that a ritual involving more equipment or fancier tools is best. This is good if it feels right for the practitioner. Some people who work magically feel that it's necessary to be magically dressed and decorated. Others do the same kind of work with nothing but a clearing in the trees. Ritual and its results depends upon the intent and effort of those using it. The deeper you can reach inside yourself to power the work, the stronger and more efficient the result. Efficiency is not a word many would bring to a discussion on magical methods, but it is an important factor. Whether one is praying or meditating, spelling or channeling, if the work you do is efficient and concise, then the results will be, too. When you do a task at work or home, you try to be efficient about it. If you do this task in a sloppy or half-hearted way, the results are less than satisfactory.

The same holds true of any work you do on other levels. If you are efficient about it, your results will be streamlined and more satisfying.

If you cannot seem to focus on the desired results of any work you do, try again another time. There are specific rituals presented in different works that are appropriate to a certain phase of the moon or season of the year. Details can be important if you use the work of another. Best to follow the tried and true instructions and perhaps modify them later at your own pace and according to taste. But generally, unless it is a specific spell, work will wait until you can empower it fully.

Working with Tea

When you drink a magical tea, you drink it for other reasons than the obvious. Perhaps you wish to help speed the healing of a friend. Peppermint and thyme would be a wonderful combination to use. Many herbs are herbs of healing and combinations are unlimited according to taste, intuition, and personal need. The peppermint and thyme will medicinally help clear clogged sinuses and bronchial tubes. If this is a need at the time, the medicinal effects are merely a bonus. The magical uses of teas are the focus here. The following tea combinations are tried and true for the fundamental needs in Tea Magic.

Caution: All herbs contain some medicinal properties and some are allergic-positive. Others are extremely harmful and should be avoided. Before ingesting any herb or combination, ensure that not only are the herbs identified properly, but that you thoroughly research them yourself. Never take one person's word on something so important. Check them out, because at the same time, you will learn and grow.

For needed income: Chamomile and Blackberry;
Sassafras and Almond;
Jasmine and Mint.

For healing: Cinnamon and Lemon Balm;
Mint and Apple;
Saffron and Fennel.

For love: Strawberry and Orange;
Raspberry and Lemon;
Licorice and Jasmine.

For purification: Peppermint and Anise seed;
Lemon and Chamomile.

When you use a tea for magical purposes, always set aside a quiet time and place to do your ritual. You should take a few minutes and run your wrists and hands under warm water. Soap them and rub them gently together to mix the energy between them. As you run the warm water over your skin, invite the power of the water to enter you for the work you are going to do. Know that the element of water is one of birth and growth, continuity and fluidity. Each of these attributes are invited into you for you to use toward the desired result.

Breathe deeply as you prepare yourself for magic. Allow the element of air to oxygenate your blood. All of the right conditions for magical work of any kind must always be brought about by proper breathing and meditation.

As you prepare the tea, enjoy the task. Don't rush to put the kettle on and hurry the burner. Really be aware of what you are doing. Hear the sound the water makes as it hits the bottom of the kettle. Look at—and really see—the steam as the water starts to boil. Enjoy the smell of the tea when you pour the water into the cup. And all the while, keep your goal in the back of your mind. The more you can associate every step in the process to the ultimate desired end, the stronger your magic will be.

Now, sit quietly by yourself and savor the taste, heat, and smell of the tea. Feel it go down your throat as you swallow. By charging (see chapter 2) the herbs or teas you are using, and by drinking their product, you are taking the very properties of them into you. Taking an herb this way enables that herb to empower you.

Never rush what you do. If you are rushing, then you only have on your mind what you must do next. It is the current moment that is important in magical work. You must see this moment as an opportunity to concentrate more fully, breathe more deeply, and accept the knowledge of that experience.

Simple teas are wonderful, as well. A simple tea is a tea made with just one herb. Raspberry tea should be a staple in every woman's home. This is not meant in a sexist manner, but rather, the tea made from raspberry leaves has properties that no woman should do without. Because women must function within the lunar cycle, the emotions and psyche can change throughout her month. Raspberry has the magical properties of protection and love. Most women experience times of stress or vulnerability through their month and raspberry is made to order. The increased protection allows us to continue work and alleviates some of the stress, by holding it at bay.

The medicinal effects of raspberry tea come into play when concerned with PMS, cramping, water retention, mood-swings, childbirth and general lethargy. Raspberry's prime function is to ease the discomfort of menstrual-related symptoms. It has been used throughout history to treat birthing, cramping, and excess bleeding. So when you feel out of sorts, or are experiencing the discomforts of your cycle, pour boiling water over crushed raspberry leaves and let steep for 2-3 minutes. Sip the tea slowly and relax. Let the herb do its allotted job and enjoy the benefits.

Cookery

Anything prepared with creativity, intent, and care is magically significant. Cooking is a dynamic field, ripe for magical uses. If you are one who uses herbs in the kitchen, the number of magically potent culinary herbs is vast. Each has its properties and each does its job when charged and willed by you. So why not use the opportunity that cooking allows.

When you are preparing food for a particular occasion, use herbs in your creations that will enhance. For example: the herb frankincense is an herb of many properties. It has protective powers, gives a balance to the spiritual aspects of the user and has a very strong use in thanks-giving. The uses of frankincense throughout history as a magical herb for burning are often noted in old texts. The bearer of frankincense to the baby Jesus was a king, therefore the gift had to befit the bearer's station in life. It has always been considered the gold of the scent and power herbs. The ancient Egyptians used frankincense in their rituals of thanks to the sun god for giving them a new day. Although it is a gum-resin, frankincense is still classified as an herbal substance because it is a plant by-product. Just as tea is infused from herbs, so frankincense is extracted from an herb.

But frankincense is not generally used in cooking. Therefore, the use of rosemary as a substitute for frankincense is common. Rosemary is an herb used for seasonings but with the potencies of frankincense. Crushed and sprinkled lightly over oven-warmed bread, Rosemary brings to your meal a joy of the occasion. It enhances the moment with protection and shows your thanks for the cause of the celebration. Celebrations of love, birth, marriage, a job, anniversaries, etc., are all occasions of thanksgiving. Use rosemary in your culinary preparations and enjoy bringing magic into your cauldron.

Basil is an herb of love, so it is used in many dishes that are often viewed as romantic. Pasta meals, seafood dishes, and salads are generally made with basil. It is used to enhance the bond between two people and should be used liberally in a meal that is designed to draw a pair closer together.

Thyme works wonderfully with the flavors of fish, yellow vegetables, and beef. It will empower your meal with strength, courage, healing, and health. Use it in your cooking the night before a test, meeting, event, etc., for added self-encouragement.

Life is about awareness. If awareness is clouded or rushed, life becomes crowded and rushed. Be aware of what you cook with. Know the herbs you use and what their properties are. Find books about herbs and their magical classifications. Learn more about the things you put into your body and discover what powers they may hold. And put their powers to work. They are there for your use. You will use these flavorings regardless. You should be aware of their other traits.

The following common culinary herbs are universally recognizable. The magical properties of these herbs is what you must know in order to complete your meal fully. Without knowing these properties, you are cheating not only yourself, but those for whom the meal is prepared. By not psychically attuning yourself to the flavorings, you are missing the extra boost your visualizations would create.

Aniseed: A sharp flavor similar to fennel in the licorice bite. This is an herb strong in protective and cleansing qualities. A sharp addition to herbal incenses for the coal.

Lemon Balm: May be used in anything which takes lemon flavor. The balm is wonderful in magical work of a healing nature and is essential in any work for achievement.

Bay: Is naturally associated with the Yule season. Bay makes a perfect base for any coal-burned herbal mixture. For a firm foundation to pursue psychic work, look to the use of this hardy herb. Bay is strong in protective work and increases the potency of any purification ritual.

Caraway Seeds: The lustful nature of the caraway is a master at increasing your desires. Use this flavorful little seed in breads, fish, or potato dishes. Best flavor when crushed in mortar. It promotes healthful color in the cheeks and energizes the personal barrier or shield.

Cinnamon: This is a flavor for matters of the heart. Love is its motivation and a deep sense of the All. Cinnamon will creep into your deeper places and open wide the windows. Airing out the cobwebs, it will freshen those places to allow them to be occupied again. Cinnamon has a happy knack of helping new love adjust itself. It harmonizes the energy between two people and enables them to know each other without awkward gaps in conversation.

Clove: Either solo or in combination with patchouli or bergamot, clove is the herb for prosperity. Its strong essence (aside from reminding us of toothache drops) will freshen the intended results in your mind.

Curry: Because of its potent ability to churn stomach acids, curry is used when one is angry or stressed. The herb evokes a feeling of tension release (physically—the perspiration is the release). But please be aware that curry is better used as a burning herb when upset, as many people cannot tolerate such a strong seasoning, or the acids caused by stress. The two can cause extreme discomfort.

Dill: Prosperity is the number one job for this lacy herb. Vinegars and oils made from dill are indispensable in the kitchen. As a base for sauces or a sprinkle for salads, dill lends its protective aspects to any moment.

Fennel: Makes a wonderful flavoring for vegetable greens, biscuits and some kinds of pastry. Its protective properties mix with your own household spirit to guard against negativity.

Garlic: Has unlimited power in the area of healing, especially in the case of heart problems. Medicinally, garlic is known for its heart and circulatory aspects and this extends to its vibratory talent as well. It is indispensable for those with "night-creeps." Children especially respond to garlic placed discreetly around their rooms. The garlic should be cut small and dried before using it as an around-the-house protective. Dried, the aroma is released only when handled. It can be sewn into small pouches with other herbs for this purpose.

Ginger: A personal favorite, ginger is an herb to be reckoned with when used for any work of success. It has a lovely scent in cookery or coal-burned.

Mace: Is used with any work of increased psyche. In any area where your powers of concentration need recharging, mace is the best.

Marjoram: Positive energy and love are the two strongest attributes of marjoram. Its fresh, sweet taste blends well with fish, chicken, and some ethnic breads. For a special dinner between lovers, or a warm get-together, marjoram will strengthen the bonds.

Mint: Is the best all-round herb. It should be added to just about everything. If the flavor is going to clash with the dish you are preparing, use a mint leaf to garnish. Its magical uses include prosperity, love, healing, and protection.

Nutmeg: Nutmeg has the happy quality of perking up the flavor of the dish it is added to. Even as a garnish for the top, nutmeg releases its sweet scent to enhance the food. Prosperity or necessity is what this seasoning is all about. If the need for money is relatively small—such as a phone or electric bill, new coat, or vet bill—nutmeg will serve your purposes well. The surprising thing about using this particular spice is the fast show of results.

Olive: Added here because of its history as a magical plant. The most common form in which the olive comes to us is oil. The olive and its refined oil were best known in ancient Greece and Rome. Athena, Patron of Athens, had as her symbol, an olive branch. The branch has remained popular in the theme of peace between warring areas. Peace is the greatest attribute of the olive.

Parsley: Used in the best purification work. Parsley has a strong flavor which goes with most foods. It has garnished plates throughout history and is a beneficial breath aid when chewed.

Pepper: Is considered the best substance for cleansing and purifying an area of evil influences or negative energy.

Rosemary: Is one of the vital herbs to have in a home. The herb itself is so handy, it could be used alone for most work concerning thanks, protection, and healing.

Sage: Personifies wisdom extraordinaire. The smell of sage is an old smell; not musty, but a full scent. The plant is full looking as well. Sage brings wisdom, patience, and learning.

Summer Savory: Makes a pleasing addition to poultry, fish, and stuffing dishes. The flavor is sweet and distinctive. Its magical capability of harmonizing the self and easing the mind of stress is easily determined. Use in a meal just before any mental exercises and check the level of relaxation you experience.

Thyme: Thyme is a healer, purifier, and a boost to psychic abilities. Its flavor in foods is changeable depending on its fellow herbs in any given recipe.

This list is just the proverbial tip of the iceburg. The variety of culinary herbs is only as vast as your imagination. Many should be used just as a seasoning, keeping the dosage to a micro-minimum. Others, such as thyme, are brewed into teas for medicinal purposes. Get to know each herb you use in the kitchen and you will find that their uses grow to other areas.

The Doorstep

Most kitchens have a door leading to the outside of the dwelling. This door either opens onto the back or side of a house, or to a hallway leading out of an apartment building. If you have a doorway in your kitchen, use betony and lavender to protect and bring peace to your home. Take equal parts of the two herbs and blend them together in your mortar. Charge them together, instead of the usual way of charging everything individually. With them blended, the charge will bond the two properties and create a stronger barrier. Clear your mind and breathe deeply for a few moments. Take a small amount and sprinkle across the doorstep. Rub a little on the frame around the door and leave some on the sill over the door. All the while, you should be concentrating on the vivid barrier. You can see it in your mind as a bright white door or a blue one. See it as distinctly as possible and hold it in your psyche for the duration of the work. If you generally verbalize your spells (or work) in some way, do so according to the path from which you work. The following incantation is one I wrote a long time ago, and it keeps on working for me.

> This doorstep with its welcome ways,
> be guarded by a shield of rays.
> To guard this home by day and night,
> protect it with this door of white.
>
> Let nothing enter not of good,
> and those within do as they would.
> The aura left by herb and spell,
> will safely seal this entrance well.

A sure way to relieve you or your home of unwanted company is to place your household broom propped beside the entrance. I have used this method on many occasions and it works! I can only assume that by knowing what the hoped-for results will be is what causes it to work. We sweep our homes with this broom, and no matter what we do magically with it, we do use it to sweep unwanted "stuff" from our space. Be it dust, animal hair, crumbs or negative energy/people, it is a tool of magic no matter how we look at it. The tasks within a home are all magical in their own right.

Magic cannot be separated from the physical things in our world or the behavior we exhibit. We must remember this in order that we may approach the moment when the world can function in harmony. By all means, set aside times and rituals, and ensure that you do your best to make these the dynamic occasions they should be. But no matter how much you plan for magical ritual, if the power of personal magic is not called into harmony with the world in which you live, then you are cheating yourself of the benefits of this union. The syncopation of the higher world of spirit and awareness with the lower world of mundane living creates a bonding of matter and energy. We have all, on occasion, gone about some task in a fog of automation. We are able to do things without thought. Most things we do in our lives have been done again and again. We pay little attention to these tasks after a time, completing them with little intellectual output. However, if we incorporate magic into these mundane events, they change dimension. Our perspective of them changes. And the purpose of the task itself changes. When we blend the force of energy with the dexterity of matter, we enter a realm of limitlessness. Allow yourself the luxury of knowing that you will never know your limits. You will keep getting stronger with your Self and the world around you. Without limits set on your abilities, you may strive for anything. You will see that the road ahead is full of possibilities and that only you can set a limit on the lessons you learn.

2

Bud, Root and Stem

he range of medicinal and magical herbs is endless. Considering the evolutionary history of this planet, I very much doubt that an herb, tree, or mold exists that does not have a practical purpose. We are not aware of every property of every herb, but in my opinion, each has a reason for being. I believe that every plant possesses a unique property that has healing power. Perhaps a cure for cancer, AIDS, or diabetes awaits the ambitious researcher in the rain forests, swamps, or fields of this planet.

Herbs are gifts from the great Mother herself. They are ours to use for healing, protection, purification and magic. We are often willing to exterminate a "weed" that looks unsightly, but in fact, a weed may be just the thing to use as fertilizer for the rest of the garden.

Each herb has its own unique vibratory energy. When an herb is used in conjunction with another herb that is close to its frequency, the power of that herb is enhanced. Herbs can be used with stones as well. Stones have energy, too. A stone and an herb of like range can compliment each other. Stones are discussed in chapter 6.

You can grow your own herbs, you can buy them at health food and herbal shops, or you can order them through the mail from different suppliers. Any method is fine. If the herbs are being used medicinally, take extra care to obtain fresh and safe herbs from your suppliers. Check out your supplier carefully before ordering. Discuss the establishment's growing and/or ordering practices, drying methods, and storage before stocking up. You will be trusting these herbs and their properties with your health and psychic well being. Make sure you feel comfortable with them.

If the herbs are purchased from a shop, look carefully to see if the color is right. The many jars of herbs should carry different tones of greens, browns, yellows, and greys. If all look very similar, perhaps your best bet would be to try elsewhere. My favorite shop is one that does not prepackage herbs, but keeps them in great jars, and customers help themselves. This way I can smell the herb, see its texture and color, and feel for moisture. When you are buying dried herbs, make sure they are dry, otherwise moisture and mildew will build up in the container. This reduces the value of the herb.

If you are unsure of anything, ask. Most people are helpful when they work around herbs. Many herbal shops also have a book section filled with herbals of all descriptions. Use them to answer your questions. Always research a remedy or simple (one-herb remedy) before you go ahead and use it. Ask someone who has experience with the remedy. Many herbs can be *very* harmful if used incorrectly. Tread lightly and experience will be yours. You do not want to make yourself sick when you are trying to heal. And *never* take the word of one reference alone. Always get a second opinion. If the herb is steadfastly known for its medicinal properties, then you will have no trouble verifying this with other authorities. With medicinal herbology, I use at least three sources for my references. If one in three carries a warning, I will go no further. Generally I will not use it if there is a substitute suggested which does not result in adverse side-effects.

Growing your own herbs, of course, is the ideal situation. Many people do not have the room, the time, or perhaps the interest to do this. However, a combination of home grown and store bought herbs can fill your herb cabinet in the most practical manner. The easiest herbs to grow at home are:

peppermint, basil, lavender, catnip, rosemary,
thyme, houseleek, parsley and garlic.

These herbs have strong medicinal qualities as well as powerful magical properties. They can be grown in outdoor gardens, but if you only have access to a balcony or terrace, these herbs will do well in a sunny spot. Their pots must grow in proportion to the size of the plant, so transplanting is a frequent venture. Good drainage and fresh soil (sandy, black, or peat) is essential because they are not planted in the earth where natural regeneration takes place continuously. Soil-strengtheners, like tea leaves, coffee grounds, and vegetable parings, can be blended in your food processor or blender with lots of water. This mixture can then be used to water your herbs and houseplants. Keep all your vegetable garbage and use it in this way. It will also help reduce the amount of garbage in your household. Store cuttings and peel in a bag in your freezer and when you have time, make up a batch of soil-strengthener.

Small bits of orange and orange peel can be sprinkled onto the top of the soil to keep mice away. And black pepper sprinkled around the stalks will deter non-productive insects.

As with balcony gardens, windowsill gardens are limited in space. If you have particularly wide sills, you can either plant in individual pots or in wallpaper troughs. These troughs are used to pull the wallpaper through the water. They are long enough and deep enough for quite a nice little garden. They do have a distinct advantage over individual pots in that the herbs which need more room can co-exist with those that don't need much room. Once in a while a pot develops root crowding or rot. But this can happen in any type of pot.

Another method for growing home herbs is using hanging pots. They have many openings down the sides, and are often called raspberry pots, vine jars, and so forth. They are designed to allow the plant growth at different levels on the pot. These are wonderful for herbs like crawling thyme, catnip, or other vine-like or trailing plants.

If you already have an herbal cabinet, you will know that some herbs are used more quickly than others. You should try to use them so that you may benefit from their potency. But if you grow fresh herbs, use the fresh ones first.

Your herbs will grow better and stronger if you provide them with a magical place. Add stones to your indoor or outdoor garden. The soft greens and browns contrast the sharp angles and prisms of light coming from crystals and gemstones. If you keep your plants in individual pots, use clay pots with drainage holes and catch-pans. The clay is a pure earthenware container and will give your plants a more natural home. These pots also belong with the colors of the foliage and crystals.

Use your imagination and create small areas full of herbs and stones around your home. When windows are closed for the winter, the small ledge halfway up is a perfect place. So is the corner of a step. Or the ledge above a door. Find the spots in your home that seem to be lacking harmony or peace and try the magical means of fixing them. It couldn't do any harm. Many people have a certain space which may not feel completely comfortable. Your home should be comfortable for you; you have invested time, money and energy into developing your environment. Each nook and cranny should feel good. This is *your* place. The place you must trust with your feelings, relationship, desires, and dreams. It should reflect the same kind of comfort to you as the friends with whom you share these things. Herbs, fresh or dried can be very powerful cleansers.

If you use dried herbs, charge them before you use them. For example, rosemary is a very potent herb of protection and purification, and it is also used for healing and psychic strength. By holding the rosemary lightly between your palms and clearing your mind and heart, you will begin to charge the herb to its purpose. Slowly pull, from your deepest place, the energy of healing. Healing is a wonderfully encompassing word. In this case we are not doing direct healing work, but any magical method that is used to correct negativity, could, and rightly so, be called healing. Here, we are healing that spot or space of energy which causes discomfort.

As you hold the herb, breathe deeply. Let each intake of breath allow you to absorb some of the herb's energy. As you exhale fully, direct your love and healing powers to mix with the energy from the herb. Feel that mixture move back into the herb. Push it into the space between your palms and let this power permeate the herb. You have charged it with your own essence, the potentiality of all that is deep inside you. The herb will vibrate at a slightly altered frequency now for a while. It still contains its own strong power, but now it also contains yours. It will combine these forces into a direct working relationship. This herb will work for you.

If you have the space to strew herbs, this method allows many herbs to work in symphony with one another. One of the best combinations of herbs for strewing is the following: lemon balm, basil, lavender, rose petals, sage, camomile and anise seed. All of them together combine to make a potent odor-remover. They each have distinctive aromas. Strewings are always better when two or three herbs are used together. My personal favorite for a delicate touch to any room, but especially the bath and bedrooms is: lavender, lemon balm and sage.

When you use herbs for strewing, charge them. The proportions in the mixture depend on your preferences. Try different combinations. When you feel that the mixture is "right," wash your hands and dry them thoroughly. Then, while taking deep cleansing breaths, crush the herbs lightly between your two palms. Concentrate on their immediate task and see, in your mind, the essence the herbs add to your home. Sprinkle them and enjoy them.

Get to know your herbs. You are trusting them to a purpose and you need to feel them before you actually use them. Before you charge an herb, hold it in your left hand and draw in some of its essence. Try as hard as you can to identify that herb through the feel of its spirit. You will come to know each one better and better as time goes on. They will all become familiar to you. This familiarity increases the bond you will have with herbs. Living things bond with other living things. All of life, animal, vegetable, or mineral is intertwined. This is the exchange of life. Life is an exchange of energies with everything around us. Living in cities has dulled our senses to this exchange.

Daily Herb Magic

Life does exist outside the circle and we must use our knowledge and abilities to enhance our daily routines. Use your imagination. Don't let your magic stagnate between circles or celebrations. That would be sad. What a waste of good time and energy. Take a few moments for magic. Magic is hugging your family one extra time, burning a few herbs for healing, and letting someone know you care. Magic comes in limitless forms; it has no one face. It begins with a notion and grows from there. It requires only that you be true in your intentions and that they will harm none. Remember the Wiccan Creed—and it harm none, do what ye will.

The life of a Wiccan is one of daily contemplation and magic. I am not saying that you *must* do ritual every day. When you do your ritual is totally up to you. What I am saying is that the everyday things in our lives can be enhanced with just a "touch" of magic. Now ask yourself, "Could I benefit from more income?" "Could I use a little more positive energy?" "Is someone I know in need of assistance?" We all can use a little help and blessings. Why not take a very few moments everyday and enhance someone's life? You haven't time, you say. Well, that just isn't true. A brief, brief moment in your morning shower, with the aid of water energy, is a perfect time to thank the Gods for the blessings in your life, and to ask for help as need be.

Hang a small felt packet of the appropriate herbs for healing, money, purification, love, etc., in your shower. Let the steam from the hot water gently and slowly release the scent of herbs in your bathroom. As you feel the water on your skin, picture the energy of the herb rising with the steam to enhance your wishes or spells. Use a few appropriate words and release the energy. It only takes a few moments, and it feels so good to use your magic to enhance your day.

We can use herbs in many ways. We can make teas, we can burn or steam them, use them as food, as pot-pourris.

Teas

Teas, as previously discussed, are used medicinally, magically, and physically. Herbal teas have potent properties. Lemon balm, for example, yields a wonderfully rich lemon flavored tea when infused with boiling water. It soothes stomach cramps, insomnia, and nervous headaches. Research it and get many opinions. But you will find when using lemon balm for the physical symptoms described above, you are also using it for its magical properties of boosting achievements and projects, increasing constructive energies.

When you make your tea, don't forget to fuss a little. Warm the pot by pouring boiling water into it before you put the herbs in. Let the tea steep and use that moment to meditate. Use your favorite cup. But all the while, concentrate on the focus for its magical attributes and properties. Bring the energy up through you to enhance the power of the herb tea. Inhale the steam, savor the taste and feel it become part of you as you swallow it. *Connect* with it.

Incense

Burning incense is a favorite for many people. I enjoy using my censer for burning the herbs I need. Mine hangs from three chains and the coals are safe. I *always* put out any coals or candles before leaving my home.

Stick incense (considered an herbal product) can be burned in a small but deep container of salt for the altar or any other spot. The salt comes from the earth and therefore can represent that element, while the incense represents air. You have combined the power of two forces into one small activity—lighting incense. *And* when you want to put the stick out for safety purposes, just push the burning end into the salt and it will be extinguished.

Steaming

Steaming or boiling herbs is a refreshing way to release their powers. Steaming in the shower, as mentioned before, is dramatic and leaves lovely, earthy scents in your bath. Boiling them in a pot-pourri kettle or other cauldron on the stove smells wonderful. The small black cauldrons are perfect for this. Heavy cast iron can't be beat for pot-pourris, for it holds the heat, and the iron, by its very nature, lends strength to the purpose. Remember, don't waste herbs, send them to a purpose. Each time you burn, boil, steam, or infuse herbs, find a good goal. If nothing comes to mind, use that opportunity to send thanks for what you have. We should do regular rituals of thanks but anytime is appropriate to be grateful for the good things in our lives.

Food

Seasoning is one area where the imagination and determination of the cook are the only things that will limit herbal uses in food preparation. Their magical properties are virtually unlimited, and they are to be used at every opportunity. As you season your recipes, keep in mind the magical traits of the herbs you use, and send that energy to someone who could use it. Each flavor-filled plant holds keys to psychic energies. When your preparations are complete, you will have enhanced the dish you are making and will have made it more potent.

Most pagans are experimenters when it comes to using different herbs in their cooking. We generally like many foods of the vegetable and fruit groups. We love new spices, and enjoy a wide range of tastes. That is not to say that this is true of all pagans. But most I meet are this way.

Breaking bread with friends and family has always been a way to celebrate the occasion. The sharing of food is a time-honored way to extend hospitality and warmth. Herb breads, fresh from the oven, are a treat for any meal and you share not only the food, but the properties of the herbs in the bread. For any herb bread, you may either bake from scratch or use unbaked frozen loaves. Just add your crushed herbs to the dough or sprinkle along the top with butter. As the loaves bake, the smell and potency of the herbs becomes one with the loaf.

Tokens and Amulets

Herbs are powerful additions to any spellwork. You will find an herb for every need. Choose which one would best suit your current magical needs and take your time to charge this herb with your own energies.

A token is literally a piece of your spell that you can take with you. It can remain on your person. If it is for a friend, they may tuck it in a pocket. To make an amulet, gather together the basic components of your altar. This list would include:

A candle of an appropriate color, i.e., green for prosperity, blue for healing or protection, etc.;

An appropriate herb, already charged;

Salt;

An appropriate incense if desired;

Your intention, written clearly and carefully, on a small, cleansed square of paper;

A small "thank-you" gift to the Gods. This could be something as simple as a leaf, flower, or drop of wine.

Do your spellwork as you normally would, using the herbs, salt, and incense dust as a mix to charge your intentions into. Don't forget to keep concentrating on your goal as you light the candle. Meditate with goodness in your heart and love in your intent.

Take a small portion of the liquid wax from your candle (about the size of a penny) and form it into a small disk with a lip around the edge. Read your spell once more and burn the paper carefully over a sink, cauldron, or in another safe place. Add a small portion of the ashes from the paper to the herb, salt, and ash mixture. Mix these together. Place a small bit of this mixture into the center of your wax disk. Flatten the mix out and drop liquid wax over it, into the disk. Smooth the wax and blend it well with the edge you left around the disk. Encase the mix in the wax token and once cooled, it can be taken with you anywhere. Tokens are pleasant to use, because as you need reassurance through your day that your magic is working, you can hold the token in your hand for a brief moment and feel the energies coming from the heart of it.

Use the herbs in your daily work. They will not disappoint you. Do your magic with all the best intentions. Never let yourself do anything that would harm anyone. Always ask yourself if the intent of your work or its results could make anyone uncomfortable or harmed. All of life's energies eventually return to their source. And by the time that return occurs, they will have gathered strength and potency. If you do harm, do not doubt the result will be that of rebounding on you three-fold.

But the same is true of good and loving intentions. They, too, return to enrich and enhance your life. Give love, you receive love. By ensuring that your actions are kind, you are ensuring your own future and the way in which people will behave toward you.

3

Mystical Flame

*E*ach of the four elements—fire, water, earth, and air—have their own mystical qualities and powers. However, fire is, perhaps, the one element that really displays it's power on a day-to-day basis. Most of the pagans I know have candles lit around their home each day or evening. Yes, the use of incense is common and frequent, but fire is relied upon to set a certain mood in the spaces set apart for Wiccan pursuits. When I think of spellwork or meditation, I automatically reach for the appropriate candle first. Next, I determine which incense would enhance my goals, but the flame of the ritual or work is considered the center for the entire practice.

Color charts very from source to source. It is not possible to say which color definitions are correct, because various teachers have had various kinds of experience with color. The following chart is my favorite. I have used these correlations for a very long time and I find them more comfortable than any I have seen. But you must use your own judgment.

ELEMENTS

Fire	—	Red
Earth	—	Yellow
Air	—	Blue
Water	—	Green

These do not, at first, appear to correspond. It would seem that water should be blue, earth should be green, etc. But these colors represent not what that element actually looks like but what potencies and powers each possesses. Red is the color of force and strength which the flame represents. Yellow is a color which has high levels of energy, and it emits this energy strongly. The Earth is a powerful source of energy and presents the element of our world. Blue is for calm and peace. It is the color for healing. It is used in highly emotional cases where the person needs to breathe more deeply and expel the negative emotions he or she is experiencing. Green is a color of growth, prosperity, and enervation. Water is a basic first necessity of life, and from water comes our ability to cleanse. To be able to cleanse and wash away the negativity, the green is allowed to enforce its powers of creativity and productivity.

These are brief statements designed to show you that the visual appearance of an element has little to do with the basic functions of the color associated with it. Knowledge regarding the appropriate use and power of color is a fascinating area of study and should be investigated if you are drawn to the subject.

BLACK: Absorbs all others. Psychic work and scrying are enhance when black is used. It is a color of inner power and the strength of the hidden Self.

BLUE: Most often used for the alleviation of emotional stress and pain. Needed for its calming qualities in spells of healing, as illnesses are empowered by negative emotions and feelings.

RED: The color of force. Not negativity but force of fortitude; the strength to fight on; the power required to give birth, to parent. A red cord for a witch's ritual wear is not uncommon, as it lends power to the work being done.

GREEN: Accomplishment, work opportunities, achievements and prosperity are all aspects of green. But in my opinion, the most important and powerful quality of this rich color range is that of perseverance. This is a trait that is needed for every aspect of our lives. Work, home, magic, creativity, and relationships all require perseverance. Green, contrary to some schools of thought, is not a shallow color relating only to money and income. Its deeper gift is the strength it gives us which allows us to continue to use our faith to keep going. The rewards are great but not necessarily income. They are a "job well done." A feeling of pride, accomplishment, etc. Green keeps us going in life.

YELLOW: Beauty is seen in the color of energy. It radiates high levels of pure energy. This revitalizing power energizes the tired spirit. It is an infuser. A yellow candle may always be used to enhance the absorbtion of spells using other colors. I often use a yellow candle in the center of my north-facing altar. There, it can represent the yellow of the earth element, the north point, and as a booster for what ever else you are doing.

REDDISH-BROWN: Is a direct representation of the lower world, the mundane, the darker corners of the cool earth. Use this color for attention, alertness, and awareness. This is the energy of the beings of the earth, the creatures who must be alert to their environment. Physical and magical alike, these creatures are aware.

PURPLE: Used when dealing with the higher powers of the universe. When thanking the gods and goddesses, when evoking direct connections to the higher beings and when needing serious and divine intervention for a healing.

SILVER & GOLD: The colors of the God (gold) and the Goddess (silver). These begin to blend in one's life when he or she begins to accept the masculine and feminine counter-traits in his or her own personality. They also represent the sun and the moon. Work with these colors on the Esbats and Sabbats.

Get to know each of the colors. Use them and begin to feel comfortable with their powerful aspects. Put these traits to good use for your home, your magic and your self. They become a part of you.

Mini Hearths & Altars

I have always viewed my altars as hearths. They emit love, warmth and magic. The hearth of any home is the "warm place," the homey place. Altars can be located anywhere and with the right energy, can express the love and warmth of a hearth. The candles, of course, provide the flame to warm the spot. The areas where you can locate them is limited only by safety and comfort. Windowsills, dresser or shelf surfaces, room dividers and headboards are all possible hearth/altar locations.

There are three basic accessories that I use to complete a mini-hearth.

1) A candle in a holder that fits with the mood of the area. For instance, if the altar is located near a collection plants or clay pots, use the small clay drain saucer from a clay pot as a candle holder to accent the plants.

2) A small container of salt, again in a complimentary holder.

3) Any form of the water element. This can include a plant (water predominant), an oil, or scent, or a dish pond using stones as an accent. The dish ponds are like tiny pools of water with pretty and appropriate crystals and stones in them to enhance the water. Even aquariums or small fish bowls are appropriate when empowering the altar with the water element.

With these three items, you have covered the four elements—water, fire, air and earth. Incense and incense burners can be used, as well any little touches to enhance your space. Keepsakes, knickknacks, pictures or handmade items, if they feel comfortable, can only serve to boost the personal power of that area. And that is what these mini-hearths are all about—personal power.

The following are suggestions for a hearth/altar for specific rooms. Each has unique features to the space in which it is located. These combinations are simple and effective. Add items you feel would build on the power they emit.

Kitchen

If you are fortunate enough to have a fireplace in your kitchen, the mantel of the hearth provides the ideal place for an altar set-up. For those of us not so lucky, locate your magical place any-where that would be safe and not encumbering your kitchen work space. A shelf, windowsill, fridge top or table can become the place of power for your kitchen area. No matter how small your space, you can always find a few square inches to spare for your magical work. Make sure the space feels comfortable to you. Whether it be a working circle or a small altar, magical spaces must feel warm and reassuring to the practitioner.

A kitchen altar could contain items such as a small cauldron for fire, water or incense coals, specific working herbs, a candle and perhaps those lovely little kitchen gnomes. These little stat-uettes are both cheerful and symbolic. Gnomes are creatures of the earth. The kitchen is the one room in a home that makes use of the earth element to its fullest. Spices, herbs, vegetables, fruit, grains, metal utensils, wooden utensils, pots and pans, clay dish-es, are all things grown or forged from the Mother. She provides us with so much in our efforts to feed and care for each other. The kitchen should be a place where thanks for these abundant gifts are given. The meals we prepare should be looked upon as offer-ings. That is how Wicca works. We give thanks and make offer-ings on our altars and the Goddess provides in kind. The rela-tionship is equal and fulfilling.

Bedroom

Hearth or altar places for a bedroom can be positioned in many places. Windowsill, headboards, dresser tops or shelves serve as a place of magic and worship. The bedroom should have an altar that reflects the quiet and relaxed atmosphere of that room. I like to use small pieces of silks, satins, or other pretty materials. They reflect the light of your candles and enhance the soft glow of the room. Use scarves if you like the fabric, or use bundles of satin embroidery threads. I softly bunch the fabric and use crystals and tokens in the center. In the bedroom, all items used for your altar should relate to love, security, passion, shadows, dreams, and astral work.

Bathroom

Your bath altar must be composed of items that will not be harmed by steam and hotter temperatures. Small votive-sized candles work well in dishes, pottery, plants (some varieties love the steam) and jar lids. Use ceramic statuary to enhance the spot. Many would think that most bathrooms yield no space to accommodate an altar. Space can be created. Windowsills, again, make great spots. But you can also purchase a three-tiered hanging copper basket. Hanging this from the shower-rod will give you not one but three areas to decorate. Grow a simple philodendron from the top basket to trail down the hanger. Use the second tier for pretty soaps and such. The bottom tier is plenty large enough to fit a candle, dish of bathing herbs, an incense burner and perhaps a decorative piece that you enjoy being near.

With a little imagination and much experimentation, you can create spaces for your magical work and pleasure. You need these areas to enhance your day-to-day life. Inner work is essential, a part of every witch's existence, but the outer person must also be fulfilled. We were given the gift of senses. It is our responsibility to experience life, so to fill all your senses is considered a thanks to the God and Goddess. To shun their gifts is to shun life and what it has to offer. Use your altars to fill your being. Sight, sound, touch, smell, and taste can all be fulfilled at personal magical spaces. A dish of salt fills four of them. A chalice of water or wine fills four. A lit candle fills four. You can see my point. It takes very little to meet the needs of our senses. Giving our senses data and input accentuates the most important sense of all when living magically. The sixth sense opens beyond this mundane world. It's power and sensitivity increase with the increase in your five physical senses. You must really know them to be able to set them aside during deepest astral or inner work. Using them helps to identify where they begin.

Doorways

In chapter 1, I gave you a very simple spell for the protection and purification of the entrance-ways to our homes. To most witches that I know, the protection spells for doors is done almost daily. Negativity does not always seep through walls. Most often, it walks through the doorways of your home, clinging to a friend. Allow your loved ones to shake off that negativity before they enter and you will never lack for laughter and love. Keep your home a castle. There is nothing wrong with a good on-going defense against the destructive forces of humankind. The cosmos gives us opportunities. Too many take those opportunities and use them for personal gain without regard for the return energies. These energies are what negativity is made from. By protecting your entryway, you leave negativity at your doorstep. You protect your home.

If you can get into the habit of doing a brief and simple ritual before retiring each night, you will find that waking becomes a greater positive experience. Your house is cleansed when you wake up and you start your day feeling brighter.

Safety Tips

Please use good judgment and common sense when using flame and burning incense.

- Never use candles or incense near draperies.
- Always have a container of sand nearby to douse any accidental spark or fire.
- Never fall asleep with candles or incense burning.
- Use great precaution if you intend to leave a spell candle lit when you leave your home. I find that the kitchen counter is safest but I rarely practice this. If I must interrupt my work, I know that the Goddess understands. I do make sure that my intentions of resuming the work are spoken as I put out the candle. Continuity is then strengthened.
- Never leave small children alone in a room with candles or incense burning.
- Use a small bed of sand or salt below candles in ceramic or glass dishes. The dish can crack from the heat of the candle.

Be very, very careful when using herbs with fire. Some spark and ignite too quickly to be safe. Care should be taken with pine needles, basil and juniper. Some also have a quality to their essential oils which is not a pleasant smell when burned. Experiment at your kitchen sink first. See which are safe and which smell pleasant. Nothing ruins the mood of a ritual faster than an accident or miscalculation.

Pathwork to the Sun God
A Journey for Men

The following is a pathworking for men. The element of fire has as its source, the Sun. Male practitioners can derive great power from the Sun—its warmth, its light, its necessity. As with any pathwork, it's better to get to know the journey before embarking. Taping it and playing that tape to yourself during your journey can also be very comfortable. Not only is the journey laid out for you, but it is presented in your own subdued voice. You direct your path and this is a better way.

As you make your way toward that place of inner fortitude, imagine that you stop to rest, seated by a roadway, leaning against a stone wall along one side of the street. It is nearly dawn. You cannot see which direction the sun rises; the sky is filled with an eerie halflight. You feel weary and in need of rest. You have experienced many dark nights. You know that today you will reach the place beyond the longest night.

You will encounter He who rules the sky. He is your father. He gives his nourishment, not in the nurturing manner of the Mother. But rather, by lighting your days and warming your soul—releasing the strength within.

You pick yourself up and continue down the stone road. The sky lightens and you clearly see your way. Your limbs feel heavy and your way is long. Further and further you go. As you travel, you notice a break in the wall beside you.

You step through the opening. Before you, spread out as far as your eyes can see, lay green meadows. Trees, wildflowers, grasses and sunshine. Everywhere you turn there is sunshine. It does not come from any one direction. The sky is ablaze with the golden mists that light this world.

As you gaze over the scene, drinking in the warmth of the sky above, you feel the cool grass beneath you. You can smell the damp earth. You hear the birds and the rustle of leaves. Breezes gently blow your hair. You feel the energy flowing back into your tired body.

Close your eyes and lie back on the grass. Drift between sleep and conscious serenity. Slowly, on the screen beneath your eyelids, see a strand of gold. Clearly see the golden sky funnel toward you. Watch as it penetrates the area of your solar plexus. Breathe it in!

This golden funnel fills the core of you with a warm flow of light. Feel it pulse deeply through your being. Allow your mind to follow this thread to it's source. You expect the sun to blaze hotly into your mind's eye but instead, the strong face of the God of the Sun stares back at you.

The stream of golden light flows from his beard. His strength and power have their source in his eyes. The craggy wrinkles tell his ancient tale. He is the Wise One, the Courageous One, the Old One.

As the stream of strength and fortitude flows through your body, each cell comes alive. Your body feels well again. Your energy is returned and you stand.

Stretch out your arms and embrace His light. Let the brilliance pulse with your body's rhythm. He is the source of strength for all that must be endured. His is the way forward through fear. From him you receive power. You see the world clearly once more. Let him into your Self, for you are he and he is you. Grasp the golden power; it is yours. He offers it to you and all you must do in return is to grow. To experience; to love; to dream.

Flame Spells

Spelling with the fire element is a powerful way to do magic. Of the four elements, fire is perhaps, the most fierce. Use the elemental for the fire realm whenever it is appropriate for your work. But please be careful in your use of elementals. They can be unusual to say the least.

The salamander of the fire kingdom is elusive and quick. It flits about like the flame of a candle. It's nature is fire. Use its qualities wisely and you will benefit; misuse them and you will get burned. When using the fire element, or it's elementals, ALWAYS use precise wording. Part of fire's nature is it's ability to travel and unless correct imagery and wording is maintained in a fire spell, the intention of that spell can go awry.

Spell for Prosperity

One green taper candle

One green thread about 14 inches long

A precisely worded spell on a small square of paper, e.g., "May I be given the opportunity to work at [specify].

The more precise and tight that a spell is written, the better the chances of it coming to fruition in the way you wish. And, as always, do not attempt to ask for more than you need. Working to win the lottery, or to inherit some substantial amount of money, I suspect is a big waste of time. Better you should realize that we can do magical work for the necessities of life and put forth extra efforts in the mundane world for the luxuries (if desired). Personally, I find that if I spell for the needs of my family, I am always provided for; either through an opportunity to write, lecture, or host a workshop. I don't have the audacity to ask for lottery winnings or windfalls. I don't want to be responsible for that kind of burden. As long as we have the necessities, I find myself motivated to work hard to achieve some of the extras.

With your candle, thread, and spell, go to your altar and get comfortable. Bring yourself to the Alpha State of psychic awareness, and breathe with a steady rhythm. Start to chant your spell very softly, over and over again. Develop a cadence. With your candle set in a good tight holder, give the flame life when you feel that you have maintained a good, steady chant.

Let the flame settle it's pace to yours. Meditate on your words; do not speak them to empty space. Once the flame has joined with you, begin to wrap the thread as close to the candle holder as possible. With each wrap, continue the pace of the chant. Say it each time you circle the candle. Do not thread it up the candle, keep it at the bottom.

When you are finished wrapping the thread, concentrate on the intentions of your spell for a moment. Do your thanks to the Gods and leave your magical place. Let the candle burn completely away. When the wax has cooled, place the ring of thread in a safe spot until your work is fulfilled. Do not forget your thanks when you dispose of the thread ritually, after your needs are met.

A Flame Spell can be done for just about anything this way. Use the appropriate color of candle, thread, and words. It is simple but really efficient. It's purpose is to enhance your psychic abilities and to put you in a frame of reference to lend the greatest energy to your work. Chanting should be a part of everyone's day. It is an excellent way to relax, get work done and re-energize.

Here are a few "old reliables" that most witches have used at one time or another:

- Carve your intentions in a spiral around your appropriately colored candle and let it burn down.

- Burn your spell paper as a part of your ritual.

- Use the wax to make a personal token as described in chapter 2.

4

Witches' Breath

erhaps the least recognized of the elements, air has many traits and can be used in many ways. Fire has its power in its more immediate aspects of heat and light. When our skin comes in contact with fire, we are very much aware! But we do not always recognize or appreciate the air element and do not generally take notice of contact between the skin and air. Unless of course, you are like me and particularly love the feel of wind through your hair. When I returned to Northern Canada after an eight year absence, I realized that one of the things that I really missed was the wind. It can be very strong; even on a hot summer day. And feeling it against your face and through your hair, is a treat. On many a full-moon night, I have stood outside and gazed upward. And many times a wind comes out of nowhere to greet me. Quietly I thank Her for the sign and I know that the significance of the air element will make itself known to me.

Oxygen is the "breath of life" and we would not exist without it. Even in the case of species (such as plants) who function on the expelled gas—carbon dioxide—their main function is to recreate oxygen from the released gases of humans and animals. Interesting to consider that Nature exists with the Law of Opposites. It works with the most amazing precision and balance. One aspect of Nature balances with another.

We can enjoy the air element in many forms. Wind, scents, herb burnings, and flame are all personalities of air. Each is an accurate representation of this element and one or all can be added to an altar or covenstead to enhance a circle or spell. But perhaps the most interesting of it's aspects is breath.

Throughout the world, ancient tales talk of the Witches' Breath. More predominant in old Gaelic folklore, the breath of witches or wise-women was said to have magical properties. She could heal a wound with her breath. She could breathe life into a newly-born babe and take breath from the dying to ease their journey to the Summerlands.

The blowing out of a candle as opposed to the pinching of a candle is preferred by many Wiccans; I prefer breathing the candle out. When I blow a candle out I *never* fail to take that tiny yet golden opportunity to re-enforce whatever I am currently working on. I ask that the smoke from my candle mix with the power in the breath that gives me life, and that my intentions are lifted to the Goddess.

Each element has an area of magical work associated with it. Air is protection, fire is cleansing, water is psychic empowerment and earth is knowledge. These, of course, overlap to a certain degree. But in general, I use this list when choosing my spells for the different needs in my work. I will focus on pulling in the power of a particular element. This allows these powers to hone in on the necessary magical need without the dilution by the other three. There are times when a mix of all the elements is best and wisest. But some spells can be written around one of the four and its focus becomes more fine-tuned.

If you have never built a spell around the powers of one of the elements, try it. It creates an interesting challenge for your imagination with regard to equipment and wording, and it causes your energy to focus itself on your chosen element. By focusing, you have strengthened the power of the spell already.

For example: You are in need of protection from particularly bad psychic energies emitted by your neighbor. He is a mean old man and has complained of your celtic folk tunes and chanting at all hours. You have tried to ignore the bad waves coming from his apartment but you really need to do something about it. You have tried to talk to him, turned down your stereo, even put up your grandmother's old quilt on the wall between your apartments. Still he complains. You have been compassionate but enough is enough. So, you can't mess with his karma and you can't spell ANYTHING even remotely harmful or negative.

Gather together the following items:

• A small square of cheese-cloth;

• Dill for its protective qualities;

• A coal and scent or a stick of incense (cinnamon and rosemary work well);

• Your breath freshened by chewing a mint leaf or drinking mint leaf tea.

Cheesecloth is perfect for Air spells. It's very porous structure allows good air flow through the magical ingredients.

Go to your magical place. Sit quietly for a moment and meditate on the purpose of your spell. Hold each item in your hands, energizing them for their contribution to the work ahead. As you picture your goal, light the stick of incense or coal. Hold the cheesecloth directly in the smoke from the incense and saturate it with the power of the air element. Remain focused on your work. Bundle the dill inside the cheesecloth and tie with a thread of appropriate color. Replace the pouch in the smoke once again. You will know when it is thoroughly energized by the scent.

Holding the pouch in your right hand, envision the energy in your body centered in your lungs. Let your lifeforce emanate from your solar plexus and let it energize your breath. As you purse your lips and ready yourself to blow gently on the packet, feel a warmth spread up your windpipe as you release the contents of your lungs. Let the power of your life-force mix with the power of the smoke and become one in their purpose.

When your work is complete, leave the packet in a dark cool spot. For this type of air spell, a root cellar, potting shed, or dark place have the perfect atmosphere to let your packet generate power. Putting it on the top of a plant, preferably under leaves to give it the dark cool effect works well, too.

Many Wiccans feel that work is not well done if all four of the elements are not represented in the spelling. If you are inclined to this kind of thinking, well and good. But keep an open mind and you could find an interesting and creative world for spelling and work by using one at a time.

For those of you who are just starting out with spelling and ritual, it can be hard to get started. If there are those around us who are not practitioners, we can feel intimidated and uncomfortable. This is precisely why EVERY witch or witch couple should have a totally private place where they can go to practice their magic in a comfortable and open way. We need that sense of privacy to fully focus on the intent of the work. Group work is wonderful and powerful, but generally day-to-day magic is performed solo. The goal of this book is as a companion volume to *Of Witches*. It's focus was to talk about many aspects of witchcraft and the solo-witch's freedom in the world of magic. This book is directed toward those who are interested in the everyday aspects of living the magic life. We can't all exist in cottages at the edge of a forest (although many of us would like to), but we can make our homes and lifestyles with a good foundation of magic.

Start with spell work. Ritual will come as you begin to feel comfortable with doing the actual work of a spell. Spelling is the "food" of the Craft and ritual is the "preparation." If you are hungry enough, you don't stop to peel the apple. You may learn with time that you prefer the apple peeled so you go through the ritual of doing that. And you may discover that you like apples both ways depending on your mood. So this is true with spell and ritual. JUST GET STARTED!

Gather your items of spelling and one by one take each in your hands for a time. Don't do anything! Just hold them. Get to know them. Try to tune into each one's vibrational frequency. When you tap in, a funny little electrical wave starts at the base of your spine and works it's way upward to the base of your neck. No matter how mild, that is a clear indication that the vibrancy rate of the object has met with yours and is recognizable as a separate power. Your senses will become more attuned and sharp and you will continue to more easily feel the difference. Trust yourself. Have a little faith and a lot of patience. Things will come to you as they were meant to. You and the Gods are one. If you trust in them then you must trust in yourself. Do the spells and the ritual will come. One day you will know what things you want to incorporate into your ritual to enhance your spell work.

Working with Air

In your magical areas, you can incorporate the element of air in many ways. One, of course, is with scent. Incense sticks are a nice tidy short burning way to scent your work. Coals (purchased at church stores) are longer lasting. A regular sized coal burns for about forty-five minutes and you can burn a variety of herbs or powders on them. They do allow you more choices during your work. Coals are very dangerous if not carefully watched. I will often light one when I am going to be in a particular room for awhile. Coals can have a bad habit of throwing sparks, depending on their age. The very old ones spit when you light them. Be careful!

My favorite place to use almost continuous incense is near my work area. When I write, I am not here. I am in whatever place or time I am writing about. Therefore, the more I can add to my writing environment to enhance that place, the greater the benefits in my writing. Especially when writing about the Craft, I use scent, music, and flame to "wiccanize" my work space. Celtic folk music is almost a must and my most-oft used sticks would be jasmine. There are times, Gentle Reader, that the writer's dreaded block gets it's nasty claws into me. Manipulating my environment helps me to build a certain type of mood to get me going again.

A truly lovely way to represent air is by creating a Witch's Bottle. An old wine bottle will do, as long as you have a stopper for the opening. Small old-fashioned apothecary bottles are great, as is any decorative bottle which suits your taste.

Cleanse your bottle thoroughly and let it charge on a functioning altar for a time. During the Full-Moon phase, at a time you are doing any magical work, hold the bottle between your hands and gently blow into it. Fill it with your breath and put the stopper in. The following night, open your bottle and light a match at the opening. Blow the match out with the sulphur and breath aimed into the bottle. The third night, drop three drops of charged water into your bottle to represent the three phases of the Moon in her water aspect.

The bottle is then ready to be used on any altar to represent the element air. It should be re-charged four times a year, for the four Greater Sabbats, the four suits of the tarot, the four seasons, the four compass points and the four elements.

Smudge sticks are a popular way to represent the air element in ritual. I find they are very popular in areas where Native North American practices are common. Here, in Northern Canada, the spiritual practices of witches is liberally mixed with traditional ways. Many incorporate Egyptian, Aztec and Norse in magic as well. The more eclectic of us use practices from our favorite traditions that have worked for us in the past, or that we are drawn to use. Smudge sticks are used in the shamanic traditions and can be made easily. They provide a blend of aromas and mix some very potent vibrational energies.

Begin with a base stick of pine or rosemary. It must be fairly sturdy and should be about a foot or more long. Branches of bay leaves, hawthorn, pine, yarrow, sweetgrass, or your chosen type are then tied to the branch with raw twine or vine if possible. I will often wrap the stick with a paper containing my spell as the first thing to be attached to my base. The other items I choose are then folded and arranged around this. The outer layer of a smudge stick should be wrapped quite thoroughly and the twine wrapped about halfway up. Hang this up by the bottom end until all of the parts are just about dry. They should not be completely moisture-free as this would cause it to flame instead of smoke. You want a bit of the essential fluids left in your plants.

When you use it in ritual, light the top end with a flame and blow gently on it to get it embered. Use it in your ritual so that it trails it's smoke about your magical place.

Of course, any spelling which involves burning the written work as part of its ritual is using the air element. The words are carried to the Gods on the smoke from the burning candle. It is rare that I would leave my spell words unburned. Unless I need them for a specific purpose in timing, I generally burn the paper after my ritual is done.

Scents—Simples and Blends

Burning herbs on a coal is one of my favorite ways to do magic, enhance the atmosphere in my home and work area, altar my meditative state, or cleanse the air.

Each herb has its own unique aroma. Raspberry leaves do not smell like perfumed raspberry incense but they are a pleasant addition to a scent burned for the safe arrival of a new baby or the speedy recovery for a woman suffering "female" problems. The leaves of plant generally do not smell like the multi-marketed perfumes that are available today. They are, however, more powerful.

If you are just starting out in the Craft, I would recommend four basic herbs with which you can do a myriad of things.

Lemon Balm: Used to flavor foods; tastes terrific in tea. Its magical properties are based on healing and achievements. These two qualities make it a good sturdy basic for any herb cabinet.

Dill: A good choice as a boost for prosperity. As a flavoring it's talents are varied. Add it to simple stews and soups during low budget times and you will find yourself receiving unexpected gifts of money.

Sage: With its "old" smell, it is a wonderful flavoring for meat dishes. It has strong properties of wisdom and learning. But tread carefully. Do not try to learn faster than you are supposed to. Sage, particularly, should be handled with reverence as it is considered one of the Goddess' strongest gifts.

Mint: One of my "stable" herbs. It is considered a condiment in my magical cupboard. I use mint to cleanse all my packets, herbs, tools, garments, and I drink mint tea to cleanse myself.

With these selections, you can do just about any type of herb magic you would like, you have four great medicinal herbs to work with for most ordinary complaints (check with very qualified herbalists if you are going to use them internally), and four wonderful simples to burn on your coals or in your fireplace.

Simples are considered any scent or herb used singly, while blends are just that; they are a blending of herbs and scents to make magically strong and pleasant smelling incense. Some herbs in combination are either overpowering or just plain smell bad.

Rosemary: A wonderful, deep smelling herb that when burned lets off a pleasant and not too strong a scent. Burn it when you wish protection or are giving thanks. Blend it with lemon balm to freshen the earthy scent of the rosemary. Lemon balm's powerful attributes of healing and achievement are a perfect match for the properties of the rosemary.

Parsley: Would work well with the dill in your packet to squelch negative energy from your mean old neighbor. The two herbs compliment each other. Dill is earthy and parsley is sweet and mild.

Mace: The herb to burn if you are doing psychic work. Mace, however, is not pleasant burned as a simple. Blend it with fennel seeds and they sweeten the mace. Fennel helps to guard against negativity while you do your work.

These are just a few examples of the ways you can blend herbs to make scents for your coals. You must go through the trial and error method like many of us because tastes vary so widely. What I like using may not be to another's taste. Try different herbs. Start by obtaining a different one each month. Through that lunar cycle, experiment and try different simples and blends. Each has its magical properties. Research these properties and blend those with compatible attributes. Try them in your burner and see.

Incense powders are available in some shops. These powders can be blended any number of ways but I prefer most of them in simple form. Jasmine, sandlewood, frankincense, patchouli (usually purchased in oil form), and myrrh are just a few of the different types available. If they are available in oil form only, the following preparations should be used to ready them for a coal. Oils are both dangerous and wasteful directly on coals.

Essential oils can be converted to incense powders in the following way. Obtain the essential oil of your choice and very fine sawdust. The sawdust can be begged from most lumber yards but you must sift this through cheesecloth or a flour-sifter to get the finest available dust.

Place a small quantity of the sawdust in a small sealable container. Drop some of the essential oils onto it and mix well. Continue to mix, adding oil as necessary. What you want to end up with is a firm unstirable consistency. It should be firm enough to pick up and shape into very small balls.

Store the little balls of oil and sawdust in the sealed container in the fridge for a few days. By cooling the oil you allow the sawdust to compact into a tighter little ball. Let them sit out open to the air for a day or two before using them. As with any remotely moist or oily scent, watch your coal carefully for sparks as you drop your scent balls onto the burner. They will emit the essential qualities of the oil using the sawdust as a combustible base.

Powdered scents are much handier but not quite as pure smelling as the essential oil. They can be mixed in any portions you desire after trying different recipes. You can also add just a touch of sawdust to the powdered mixture as a filler. Often a scent is just too potent to use alone and the dust helps tone it down.

Offerings and Thanksgiving

You may wonder why I would include a thanksgiving section under this particular element heading. What, you might ask, is significant in rituals of thanks that are related to air? Air is the element of the East in a circle. East is the direction of beginning. The Sun is born to our world every morning in the East. And air is the Breath of Life.

As we give thanks, we are in fact, acknowledging an occurrence in our lives which has been beneficial to us in some way. Whether the occurrence was positive or negative is not important. What is important is that you understand the reason you are giving thanks for gifts received. That acknowledgment of the lessons learned or the gifts received is, each and every time, a new beginning. It is a new you moving forth from that ritual of thanks. A more enriched and knowledgable you. With that knowledge comes power. And with that power comes a grave responsibility. So each time, you grow, and change.

This constant rebirth of our spiritual selves is why I feel that air is the perfect element to represent a ritual of thanks. The following is a simple ritual to express thanks for the lessons your life has offered you. It is one that I use fairly frequently because of it's very personal nature.

Ritual of Thanks

Set your altar to face East if possible. This ritual does not require much equipment so a small workspace is all that is necessary. Use the following items or substitute as you see fit according to personal taste.

One blue candle;

Three kernels of unpopped corn;

One apple cut on the cross, showing the pentagram inside.

Light your candle with the following words:

"Great Goddess, Lady of the Summerlands, Mother to us all. I welcome you to this place of power and offer thanks to you for what you have given to me. I am a priest(ess) of your path and I see with your eyes. You guide me to the lessons I must learn."

Put the bottom half of the apple in front of you on the altar. Charging the three kernels of corn between your hands, repeat:

"As the Maiden is ripe with potential, so is my life.
As the Mother gives birth, so do my thoughts.
As the Crone nourishes life, so do I nourish mine."

Place the kernels in the center of the core-pentagram and melt wax from your candle to cover them. Replace the top of the apple while the wax is still warm. Leave that apple sit on your altar for three days and nights. At the end of that time, remove your wax token and bury the apple. If this is not possible for some reason, you can leave it in an area near trees or shrubs where the fruit will once more become part of the soil. The wax token can remain on your altar as long as you wish.

Purifying and Energizing

As I mentioned earlier in this chapter, mint is a very potent herb for purification. It's particular astringent qualities make it the best choice for mild internal cleansing. Use the pre-bagged mint teas available where most caffeine free teas are sold. If you are going to use it for magical purposes, make sure that it is not a blend. Many of the teas sold are blends which, although tasty, are not focused enough for magic.

Mint grows quite freely in many yards and gardens. Because it regenerates itself every year, the more you cut during its peak season, the better your crop will be the following year. When you cut mint make sure you wash it thoroughly. Because of it's leaf composition, it attracts dust. Soaking it in a sink of cool water for a few minutes, is the best way to start. Rinse it carefully and use the leaves at their freshest. The stalk and stems can be dried and powdered as a base for many herbal incenses. Extra leaves can be moistened, laid out on a piece of wax paper, frozen and used individually as needed. These frozen leaves can float in a cup of tea, garnish dishes, decorate breads, etc.

If you are going to dry any leaves, hang them while still on their stalk, root end up. They can dry in any area of your kitchen that is moisture-free. When the leaves are dry, store them in a non-clear, glass container in a dark place. If the container is well sealed, their potency will last for about six months. These dried leaves can be sparely sprinkled on fish dishes. This adds a subtle but unique flavor. Use it with plenty of lemon. The two tastes really compliment each other.

Mint powdered can be added to any incense, tea, spell packet, token or ritual and it will gently purify your area, tools, spirit or body. It is not a "mighty" herb but rather, quietly very potent.

There are many herbs whose properties include purification, but few whose vibratory energy is compatible with so many others.

One of my favorite ways to begin spell work or ritual is with a gentle cleansing of the entire area including tools, etc. Once the altar is ready to go, whether or not I am building a circle, I light my coal and burn four mint leaves (four pinches if it is powdered). I am purifying my magical world and its four directions. Everything within that space gets a thorough psychic scrubbing and the mint-smoke disperses any residue negativity.

When approaching the tasks of purification and energizing, one must be very careful to be fully aware of what energies exist in the atmosphere of your magical place. Residual energy from previous spells, negativity from disuse of the space, emotional (dis)harmony and your state of mind all contribute to the balance or imbalance of that place and the things in it. All solid items in our mundane world vibrate at a particular rate. If that vibration ceases, as it does with the death of a person, animal, etc., the object or body will begin to decompose and eventually turn to ash.

When you do a purification, which should ALWAYS precede an energizing, you must tune yourself into the various frequencies and characteristics of the energies around you. Once you have done a "cataloging" of these frequencies, you are then able to attune yourself to the negative ones and balance their emission. This will bring your area into harmony. But these negatives sources must be taken care of. Only then can you proceed to purify the necessary things.

Witches use different methods of purification. I use the air element a great deal, depending on the work that I am doing. I use the other three for very specific things, but generally I find that incense allows me a hands-free approach. Once I have balanced my altar area, I light my incense and let the smoke move about the space on its own course. I might then brew myself a cup of mint tea and cleanse myself as well. The smoke permeates the area and has a "smoke-house" effect. All is cleansed and free from negativity.

For a general energizing method, turn to your Witch Mirror for help. Mirrors are normally associated with the water element but that is usually because of their reflective qualities. The atmosphere on the other side of a looking glass is described in old fables and myths as a world of air. Not as nothingness, but of the realm of the sylphs. They can sift about freely in this world and go unnoticed to the untrained eye.

A Witch Mirror is any particular mirror that a witch uses either for scrying or for glimpses into the Eastern realm. Choose a mirror which really "feels" right vibrationally. Decorate it as your taste dictates. But you should store your mirror, when not in use, wrapped in black material (preferably natural) in a box. You can design or decorate the box, etc. Your mirror is your gate to the world of sylphs; just as your cauldron or grail is the gate to the water realm, fire is the gate to the fire realm and sand or salt can be the gate to the earth realm.

Your mirror, when used for energizing, will increase the strength of the energy you put into this work. To use your mirror for this purpose, place in front of you flat on the altar. Ready yourself with the appropriate breathing and meditative exercises and concentrate on your solar plexus. This energy source in your body tends to emit the strongest vibrations of your personal strength.

As you gather energy in this spot, try to visualize the energy as a certain color. Whatever color feels comfortable is the "right" color. When you have gathered a good supply of your energy, release it from yourself. See it in your mind traveling over the mirror on the altar. As it does, the energy doubles. One stream moves from you, the other from your mirror. This is not merely reflected energy, but a doubling of your psychic efforts by using your mirror. And the additional stream of energy is directable just as is the one emanating from you.

Air magic can be accomplished in so many ways. I have talked at length about herbs and incense and their uses in spells and rituals. But these are not the only forms that air magic can take. Hand gestures and movements are a part of air magic. As you circle your hands over your cauldron, as you wave to someone, as you point to something, your hands are following the movement of sylphs. The more that you become aware of these finer points of perception, the more they become a chance for conscious magic.

Dance and body movement are also movement of the sylphs. Use your favorite music, lighting, and magical space. Begin to meditate at your altar. Most human beings have been conditioned to know that there is a precise and appropriate place for things like dance. You must make yourself understand that it is OK to move while being in your hearth-spot. If you feel like moving or dancing or drumming, do so. This is your place, your time and your psyche. You are in control of this place. If dance is something that helps you to attune yourself to the music of the cosmos, then by all means. Swaying, stepping, and circling are helpful in that they begin a certain rhythm for you. You become a part of that rhythm and your psyche is much more powerful. Chanting or drumming does this as well. Breathing is a rhythmic activity and we, as travelers in life, can use that rhythm to our advantage.

Sometime, on a hot summer night, build yourself a circle and place a fan set on low, in the East. Have it blow gently through your magical area and feel the air move around you. Skyclad (naked) or gowned, this feels wonderful. Because the area outside the perimeter of the circle is generally quite dark, you do not see where the breeze is coming from. Use covered candles or set them higher than the height of the fan. And most of all let your imagination run free. Let the wind move through your hair and cool your skin.

Wands

Debates abound regarding the elements of fire and air and their corresponding magical tools. You may be able to find both points of view in your bookcase right now. Some witches feel that the wand is a tool of fire and the sword a tool of air. My personal feelings on this matter are the opposite. My wands work for me as a tool of the East, of air. My athame and sword are both tools of fire and I derive great power from them in this capacity.

I have many types of wands. I have one I made years ago for myself. I carefully burned the appropriate symbols into it and finished it with sealant. I have a few that friends have given me along the way. But my favorites are those which my daughter Kelly has gathered for me. She has spent hours stripping the bark and cleaning a birch branch for me. These wands are the most beautiful I have, and once they are cleansed and consecrated, they are a delight to use. One is about five feet long, and presents itself as almost a staff. Another is just the length from my elbow to the tips of my fingers. This is a suggested length if you wish to make your wands. If you do not have one, be patient. Like all else in the cosmos, one will come to you when you have need of it. I had gone out to walk through the park near my house when I found my first one. It's length was perfect and it had a natural handhold that fit my hand as though it were made for it. And indeed, I believe it was. It came into my magical life at just the right time. It put a whole new perspective on my work. It expanded the possibilities and I have used it off and on for years. It's energies are comfortable and precise.

When you use your wand, don't hold it as though you are afraid of it. It is your tool. It should become an extension of your arm. Use it's tip as though to direct energy and in fact that is precisely what you are doing. See the energy coming from it. Envision it in your mind and hold your focus. You will feel the wand's power as it travels up your arm and blends with your own life's energy. Aside from invoking and banishing pentagrams, gestures used with a wand are basically up to the practitioner. Comfort is a big part of what you will do with this tool. Begin small and you will find that your attunement to the wand becomes strong. You will find yourself picking it up from it's regular spot to hold and draw energy from or to stir the air above your spellwork, cooking, etc.

> Walk with me on a windy night
> and let your heart roam free
> run through waves of silvery light
> take my hand . . .
> explore with me.

5

Water's Edge

O ur dependency upon the four elements is total. Each, in it's role in the drama of life, contributes to our survival as a species. And as siblings in this great and thinking genetic goulash, we are each striving to enhance our little corner. Unfortunately, a more global view must be seen. Steps have been taken to clean up the mess of the 20th century, but we are not there yet. Our awareness of this great dependency on the Mother Earth and Father Sky is paramount to our survival.

I am not particularly fond of metaphors, but they do have their place. And here if something to ponder: consider our average homeowners. They have purchased a piece of this planet and are ensconced comfortably within. You go to the door and inform them that they must, in the future, dump all refuse, papers, dirt and dust in the middle of their own livingroom. How appalled they would be.

This mind set has developed into two distinctly different paths. On one hand we will fight to the death to preserve our homefronts; "man's home is his castle," etc. What we have purchased, we protect. But how can we purchase a piece of something without the awareness that the rest of that something exists? Especially when the rest is attached to our own purchased piece. Where does this thinking come from? It is not OK to soil our own homes, but it is OK to soil our communal areas.

We need our world and we need each other. It really is that simple. If we could go forward from that thought, think of the difference. Idealistic impossibilities, perhaps. But we have to come to some understanding. Our world depends on it. I am not idealistic enough to think there will ever be a time of total global peace, or reduction of pollution to zero, or the complete disarmament of every nation. But the way I see it, the greater our magical and practical efforts, the closer we come to achieving even just a little of that dream. The important things in life must be undertaken one step at a time. The little things do count.

Water, Water Everywhere

The Earth and the body are one. Each has its vast store of knowledge and memories. Divinity is within both and without both. Each is composed of molecules, atoms, and particles. Each has its sophisticated processes which, so far, the human brain has not been able to decipher completely. And each has survived because of its basic elements.

Water is everywhere. Our bodies are majority water. The Earth is majority water. Tears, rain, blood, and birthing fluids are all fluids of life. They are forms in which water plays a key role in our lives.

Water is one of the most interesting of the four elements because of its ability to present itself in different states. The other elements do this, too, but the states of water are much more noticeable and useful. Water can be used in a liquid state, solid state, or gas. And for magical purposes, all the states of being are wonderful tools for spell work. The following are three simple spells for each. The intent is not important so long as it is positive. These exercises will enhance your awareness of the states of water, and you need only have a good and simple goal in mind while working them. Choose the appropriate colors for any equipment you might use, according to your work.

Ice

You will need:

> One ice cube;
>
> One piece 18" thread.

Get seated comfortably in your magical spot and place the cube in a dish large enough to hold the water in liquid form. Focus on the intent of your work and charge the thread between your hands. Breathe deeply and rhythmically. Once you are in a relaxed frame, start to wind the thread around the ice cube, moving in a clockwise direction (doesil). As you wind, keep a steady, slow rhythm and clearly see your goal in your mind.

When you are finished winding the thread, thank the Gods and close your magical space. Leave the dish on your altar and when the ice has completely melted put the put the ring of thread in a safe place. Dispose of it after the work is complete. Drink the water from the ice cube and picture the magic of your spell becoming one with the magic of your body.

Steam

You will need:

> Boiling water;
>
> Spell written on a strip of cloth.

Stay at the stove and let the water continue to boil. Again, with the intent of good, focus on your goal and breathe yourself into a relaxed state. Take the strip of cloth and pass it in the steam above the pot. If your cauldron is stove-worthy, use it. The association with the water element would enhance the spell. Use a good long strip of cloth for this so that your hands will stay out of the steam. Steam burns can be dangerous. Be careful.

When you feel that the time is right, thank the Gods, roll the strip of cloth into a tight package and place it on your altar. Once the work is done, burn it in your ritual fire.

As you do work with these different states of water, consider the versatility of this element. Use your senses to really see the magic of this trait.

Liquid

You will need:

> 5 oz. clear water (preferably purified);
>
> Eyedropper bottle half-filled with black ink;
>
> Pinch of the appropriate herb.

Sit in your magical place and breathe yourself into relaxation. Pour the water into your cauldron or other receptacle. Gaze into it and see your goal. With the eyedropper, drop seven drops of the ink into the water at different places. But here's the trick: as you drop each onto the surface of the water, watch it swirl, and blend. See the depth of the water increase. See the deepening of your spell as each drop becomes one with the water.

When you have finished, float the herbs on the surface. Let this sit on your altar for a full seven days. Dispose of the contents of your cauldron in running water.

These spells can be totally modified to your taste and creativity. But the important thing is your increasing awareness of the states of water. These also show that spells do not have to be complicated to work. They can be simple and easy and quite effective.

Really work at getting to know this wonderful element. It's movement, cleansing powers and life-giving energy will greatly enhance your life. Be thankful for it's abundance. There are many places in the world where five ounces of water are more precious than gold. Learn to appreciate this gift and use it in your everyday magic. See your own beginnings in this element. We come from a world of water. We are familiar with it by memory. Recapture this memory and it's power will aid you in your work.

Baths

There is no feeling quite like that of climbing into a steamy tub scented with relaxing herbal fragrances. As the heat eases the tension from your neck, try to picture the incredibly strong magic that this atmosphere could produce.

Think about the entire ritual. And indeed, that is what it is. When we do something with a specific intent, we have ritualized those actions. In this case the intent is the feeling a hot bath will produce in you. Anticipation is what causes ritual to come alive. Every gesture and movement is designed with one end in mind. From taking your clothes off to running the water to adding a scent or bubble to lighting a candle. Whatever your preparation, you are readying yourself for the experience of the bath—psyching yourself up, so to speak. We must ready ourselves to accept what comes our way when we are stress-free. Stress is a wonderful tool to keep thoughts at bay. We are so concentrated on the source of the stress, we seldom have time to allow new and constructive thoughts in. But when we relax and become relatively stress-free, we are open to these new and interesting thoughts. We learn much in a half hour soaking. Our mind is free to wander and pick up stray messages we should be listening to. When our mind is open to unlimited possibilities, our lives become open as well. If we limit our choices of thought, we limit our lives. As long as we retain the power to envision the scenes of our life, we can shape our paths. We need only have faith in ourselves and the Gods. The rest will come.

I try always to use a pinch of mace somewhere in the bathroom during a steamy shower or bath. Mace is an herb which gets to the root of psychic activity. It evaporates the heavy veil surrounding your psyche. You will find that your concentration increases significantly. Your thoughts will not jumble or appear to be vacant or unimportant. Your bathing experience will be stronger for using mace. It need not be burned to work. Actually its energies increase while absorbing steam. A sprinkle is usually more than adequate.

As you prepare yourself for the bath you have drawn, keep your intended goals in mind. Do not avoid your own reflection. Many people do. Pay attention. Mirrors are terrific conductors of psychic activity. They can be somewhat frightening in certain lights. Especially so for small children. When you have a candle lit, be careful about inviting your littlest children into the room. A large mirror, candle-lit, can distort all the images the child sees.

Take a few minutes before you bath to spend energy on yourself. Use body lotions and gently rub it into your skin. Feel the muscles start to relax and send energy waves to your pulse points. Concentrate the force through your palms and feel it connect the vertebrae up your back. That tingle at the base of your spine will be a strong indicator of connectedness. Pay attention. Gently but firmly rub the lotion into the areas of your back, shoulders, arms, legs, and torso that you can comfortably reach. Don't strain. That defeats the purpose.

Do close your eyes and feel what is going on in your body as you redirect the energy back to yourself. Just as a battery needs recharging, living things need recharging. By rubbing your hands over your skin, you direct the constant flow of force from your hands to your body and psyche. As you massage in a circular motion, softly chant your spell. Make everything rhythmic. Your hot bath will lock in the moisture and your skin will benefit.

Use herbs that are appropriate to the work you are doing. As you choose them, keep in mind their fragrance. If they are not an appealing bath herb, place them in a dish or around your candle. Their absorbtion of the steam will be sufficient to release their power. Make sure you charge and crush them before you use them. Or you can combine these herbs in a packet made of cheesecloth and hang it by a cord to the bath tap. You can even toss the packet right in the bath. Make sure you are not allergic to any of the plants.

As you soak, consciously feel the tension drain away. Your neck area will be the most important for it's capacity for storing tension is beyond bounds. Ours necks take the brunt of stress. We may not realize this but it is quite true. The shoulder muscles, the spine, neck muscles, and the muscles at the base of our skull all store negative energy. We must concentrate very hard to release our muscles of their burden. And most of all, we must give ourselves permission to relax. That is the key to the whole thing. One must realize that it is OK to stretch out and release all that pent-up stress. We don't need it. We can definitely survive just fine without it. But the sad part is that many people are incapable of doing just that. They have been conditioned and "functioned" into beings who must take all the troubles of the world upon their shoulders. Chances are they have felt responsible all of their lives. No one ever told them that they didn't need to be responsible for others behavior. No one told them that each person is solely responsible for his or her own behavior. Each of us must answer for our own behaviors.

The following are some simple herbal recipes which you can try. Each is safe unless a specific allergy exists.

In the bath: For tired muscles, use pine, juniper, thyme, lavender and rosemary.

For relief of depression, use rose, geranium, lavender and patchouli.

For relief of stress, use lemon balm, rose, jasmine, sage, and lavender.

For a hair wash: To shine and protect, use juniper berry, lavender, and rosemary. Mix these ingredients well in your mortar and boil in water. Strain and use after conditioner. Do not rinse. Towel dry.

A skin wash: For scrapes and heat rashes, use peppermint, verbena, thyme, and lemon balm, or a simple made from any of these. Combine equal parts if using combinations and boil down. Strain and wash effected area with the concentrated liquid. Store extra in a glass container in the refrigerator.

Each of these is a water-based substance and each has unique healing properties. I truly wish that more people would take the time to research and study the power and properties of herbs.

Movement and Light

The combination of candlelight and water has always fascinated me, and I know that I am not alone in this. When the Moon shines on the surface of a lake, the night takes on extraordinary power. When your candles gleam on the surface of a still bath, you can feel the power of the two elements.

One of the prettiest effects from candlelight comes from floating candles. There are two kinds of floaters. One is a candle shaped like a small, fat disk which, when lit, floats on the surface of the water in your tub. It burns into the center so that you can use it for a fair bit of time. These look lovely floating in your tub when you have guests. A small bit of water and a few drops of pretty vegetable food coloring and your powder room takes on a new atmosphere.

The other kind of floating candle is made from a small plastic dish into which you insert a wick. You then add a layer of cooking oil to the disk and the candle floats and burns the oil. These are a fussier type but shine a beautiful light. Each can be burned for a long time, and each is harmless when floating in your tub. Because the wick is centered in the candle, the flame can never actually touch you if you are bathing. The edge of the candle hits your leg and moves in the other direction. Quiet meditation is wonderful in a hot bath surrounded by candlelight.

Floating candles can also be used during circles for different seasonal festivals which I will discuss in chapter 7. Float them in your chalice or cauldron. On your altar or around the circle, they cast a mysterious light to enhance your work or celebration.

The movement of water can be a great help in your work. Considering it's hypnotic motion, moving water generates more energy. You can use your breath and blow to create ripples. The rings of water move in an outward direction from the source of the breeze and as you watch the ripples, repeat your goal in a rhythmic manner. Let each set of waves die away before beginning another. Each has its base of power and the power will direct itself at your specified intent.

Of course, the ideal would be to have access to a shallow pond or pool in which you could create a life-sized whirlpool effect. I remember creating these in our backyard pool when I was a girl. My friends and I would circle the pool round and round. Pushing the water in front of us, we eventually got enough momentum going to cause the water to continue to swirl. We, of course, did not know that the power created from such movement charged all of us with energy, but we knew we enjoyed doing this. Now, as an adult and Wiccan, I understand that the power I create with water movement can enhance my spells or my own sense of well-being.

When I am in the bath, sometimes I will take a very light scarf with me and make patterns in the water with it. Trailing it around the surface of the bath can create movement that compliments the gentle spell work I am currently doing.

Exercises done in a pool are extremely beneficial to anyone doing them. Older people help the pain of arthritis, and muscle aches. Physically challenged people and children are learning the benefits of water movement. Even babies benefit from pool therapy. Babies seem to have a natural inclination to dog-paddle and they adjust to water fairly quickly. They have just recently left a world of water and to be buoyant again must feel wonderful to them. Elderly people benefit from the buoyancy of water when the movements may have been too difficult for them without that buoyancy.

If you have the opportunity to do so, while in the water, move with your spells or intentions. Let the water soothe and protect you. Let it energize you and surround you with it's power. Move freely and to your own feelings. Let your body use your own inner vibrations to move and blend with it.

Water should be utilized with care. Our environment cannot continue to be used up as in the past. We must use it wisely and reuse it when possible. Unless you have used shampoo, rinse, or bath oil, the water from your herbal scented bath becomes a perfectly acceptable substance with which to water your household plants or garden. Fill a few milk or pop containers with the water and let it sit in a cool place. Most of the minerals and pollutants will settle to the bottom and the water can be used. Leave the bottom inch or so. That is where the concentration of non-useful substances will be. You can also recycle bath water, even if you have used shampoo or bath salts, by using it for cleaning. Store it in any container and when you need it, just add your cleaning product. Many times, baking soda or vinegar will suffice as a cleanser.

Purification with Water

Water purification is a unique and simple way to cleanse the tools of your work and yourself. By washing before a ritual, you are revering the Gods as they should be revered. First, you are caring for and maintaining their precious gift to you—your body. This functioning unit is a miracle in its structure and maintenance. Each part, seen and unseen, works in harmony with all others. Its perfection cannot be measured, and we are still learning more about its miraculous systems.

Second, you are washing away negativity so your ritual (or spell work) is generated in a more positive environment. Many religions of the world insist on ablutions prior to prayer. There is no rule in the practice of witchcraft that says you MUST bathe before your circles, but it is always a good idea, if possible. At the very least, you should wash your hands and temples. If you plan to wear makeup to a Sabbat or Esbat, do your ritual ablutions prior to putting it on.

As you rub your hands together, feel the energy circling your hands, moving up your arms, across your shoulders, and back to your hands. The stronger this circular motion of energy is, the more positive your force is. As you wash, you should be able to feel the path open up and the energy flow getting stronger. Pay attention and your awareness of this will increase.

I have stated numerous times in both *Of Witches* and this book that awareness of the states of energy is the most important aspect to any work or celebration. You need to be as aware as you can because the outcome or answers to your work will only be at your disposal if you are aware of them when they come. If you are not, then you could miss them and the opportunity to achieve what you were asking for. The answers rarely come to us in big, neon letters. Rather, they appear to us in subtle ways. We can miss the symbology if we do not look carefully.

The nicest part about being aware of the energies you have is that, with increased awareness, you become more attuned to your work and environment. This becoming in tune, results in a greater understanding of your needs and those of other people. This understanding, in turn, enables you to be of a greater benefit in aiding people who need your help. The cyclical patterns of energy emission and return are a composite part of our existence in the mundane world. We need to follow them and enhance their strength in order to use them wisely in our work.

Running water works well for cleansing purposes. To save stress on our water supply, use a large cauldron or bucket, and scoop the water up and over the item being cleansed.

After the cleansing is completed, please do not throw the water outdoors. It is full of whatever negativity or old work that came from your tools. Instead, set it on your altar or in one of your magical spots. Leave it for a cycle of seven days, or one aspect of the Goddess in her moon phases. This will serve to purify the water, after which you can water your plants or dispose of it outdoors.

Letting an object sit in water is another good way to cleanse it. So long as the object will not be harmed by being soaked, keep it in the water for three days. If possible, set it in a window which can pick up the moon's rays, and this will aid in the cleansing process. Candles do beautifully purified in this manner. You can do more than one at a time provided it is only a cleansing and there is no intent involved other than that purpose.

Always keep purified water on your altar. Any aesthetically pleasing container will suffice to hold a small quantity. But you can be sure that just when you get into the ritual or work you are doing, you will realize that a thread or coin or some other object that you are working with has not been cleansed. In this case, the water will be right there where you need it. Drop three drops of the water on the object and evoke the power of that element to cleanse your item. Because it has a regular place on your altar, this water is particularly powerful and the three drops represent the three phases of the Goddess in her Lunar aspect. The moon rules water. This can be seen in the Lunar tides. The correlation of tides, the lunar cycles, and a woman's menstrual cycle will be discussed in detail in chapter 7. But for our purposes here, any symbology relating to the moon is appropriate for most water work.

Cleansing or purifying with water brings out the strength of the item or person. Each element evokes specific traits when used to purify. Fire draws forth courage and raw power; air highlights the merciful and beneficent traits; earth enables the philosophical and metaphilosophical thought patterns to emerge; and water embraces the traits of strength and birth/growth. When cleansing and blessing your implements and your person, keep these traits in mind. As I said earlier, many instances call for purification by all of the elements, but in much of your simple work and individual daily spells, use of one relevant element can be appropriate.

When cleansing anything, keep focused. Do not let your thoughts drift, even if the cleansing process becomes so familiar that you must work at paying attention. Do concentrate. Your intent in maintenance of your magical pieces is as important as any work you do with them. As with anything, care and upkeep is necessary to derive the maximum power output you can have.

Water Gazing

Scrying in a cauldron or container of water requires practice and perseverance. One does not usually bingo on the first attempt. If you persist and continue to remain aware, you will eventually be successful. But you must also be patient. If you allow frustration to cloud your psyche, you will impair your growing ability to scry clearly.

When beginning this activity, start simply. A black or dark bowl of water is best. Begin with a large opening on this container. Give yourself a large viewing screen, so to speak. After you have become proficient at this, your gazing surfaces can be decreased in size without inhibiting your abilities.

If you do not have a container which has an inside surface that is dark, use ink or a mixture of food coloring to achieve the blackness of a deep water surface. You want to be unable to see the bottom of the bowl by gazing at the surface. By darkening the water, you can create the illusion of bottomless depth.

Use candlelight to light the area where you are scrying. You will need a candle fairly close to you. But not so close that the flame is reflected in the surface of the water. You can look past the reflected shadows but a distinct light could be difficult to disregard when gazing into the water's depth. Later, when your abilities have been sharpened, you can try beginning your scrying with deliberate bonding to a flame reflected in your cauldron's surface. But to start, better if you eliminate as many possible distractions as you can.

Breathe yourself into calmness and relax your spine. Sit comfortably with the container in front of you on a table. Place your hands on either side of the pot, resting with the palms facing your scrying water. As you relax and let your thoughts drift randomly, gaze into the water. Feel the energy flow, encircling your arms and shoulders as I talked about earlier, only this time the energy circle includes the bowl of water. You have now invited this piece of magical apparatus to become part of your force. This cyclical movement of the energy between you and the scrying surface is what will eventually bring the forces into alignment and cause you to "tune-in" to what can be seen in the water's surface.

As you gaze, slowly bring your thoughts into focus. Don't let them drift any more. Maintain a rigid concentration on the water's depth. See yourself slowly blending with the liquid. Your body is surrounded by warm water. You are floating, gently drifting along on the black surface. Let yourself go to this mystical pool. Allow yourself to become one with it. It encircles you as securely as the waters from which you came. Keep your focus, but let your body give itself over to the relaxing buoyancy of the water. Effortless and free.

Now sharpen your focus and draw back from the water's black sheen. Gaze deeply into the pool which you just visited. See into its depth. Allow the images to rise to the surface. See them in your mind. You will not necessarily see a video-like image on the water, but the water will help to clear your mind's eye, and will cause the images to show themselves. You will start to piece these images together. You must trust your instinctual interpretations. What feels right as a translation means you are on the correct path. But leave the interpretations for when you are finished scrying. The first few times you try this, you may want to record the session or have a friend take notes. You cannot be expected to attempt new magical abilities and remember everything that you describe seeing, as well. You will become good at remembering what you see, and in what order, but don't expect too much from yourself at first. Be patient!

As with many other forms of scrying and divination, water gazing must be interpreted less literally than symbolically. Many gazers use similar interpretations as in dream analysis. But each practitioner must use whatever methods are comfortable. If you do not feel right with the symbology pieced together one way, try approaching it from another. I am by no means saying that you should rewrite what you see. Rather, you have the option of reworking the symbols as you would an anagram, just as when we read the tarot, we can get off track and need to rework the card's imaging.

If you have on occasion had successes with this method and seem to be having a "dry spell" lately, try tossing scrying herbs into the water a little at a time. Pay attention to the pattern of the herbs on the surface of the water, and to the water, itself. See the images as a whole rather than parts of the surface. Sage is a must for most Seers I know. It is the herb of wisdom, rather like the owl of the night forest. Mace and thyme are both herbs of psychic improvement. As mace is generally powdered form, use this last. It will coat much of the surface so give the others a try first. A mere sprinkle should be enough to stir the cosmic waters.

SEEKING WISDOM

Lady of the Lake
as you stir the waters
remember me.
Your cauldron deep
your power fierce
protecting all who serve.

Let not the night be wasted
as we dance among the stars
seeking wisdom.
She will guide and nurture
if you keep to the path
with love in your heart.

Seek only the light
not shadows that mislead
but knowledge which will free.
The chains of truth
will stoke the fires once more
burdening those who decree.

6

Crystal Clear

alk with me through the cool, green forest. The sunlight dancers play as we go deeper into the woods. The path is narrow and tangled with roots. Step carefully; you wouldn't want to miss this journey. Smell the moss that grows in the dark, damp places beneath the trees where the earth folk dwell. See the shimmer of leaves as the sun begins it's decent. The forest comes alive with the nighttime sky. Her creatures peer from around tree roots and mossy mounds. But do not look for them. They choose to remain unnoticed until the time is right. If you prove worthy, perhaps they will allow you a glimpse tonight.

Feel the trunk of that tree. How rough it looks, but it is smooth to the touch. The bark of that tree has potent healing powers, but that is for another journey. Tonight is for reaching the Morrigan. The great and mighty mother whom we call Earth. She is the cool, dark mistress upon whom we rely for our very survival. The journey will be enlightening. Your eyes are opening to the life-giving forces of the mother. You are becoming aware of what she gives to us and what we must do to fight for her honor. We are Her champions. We must continue the quest and strive to preserve Her.

Sit with me on this fallen tree trunk. We will dine on rolls and cheese. The wine is chilled by the cool of dusk. Here, quench your thirst, friend. You will need your strength if you are to learn to connect and be one with the Morrigan. She is no gentle partner. She commands the creatures of her belly—the nightwatchers hidden in the dark places, those who dwell in the nooks and crevices beneath the great oaks.

Drink fellow traveler, for you will greet the morning with surety in your heart. You will know Her and feel comfortable with your connection to Her. You will work Her magic. You will seek Her guidance. You will call forth Her creatures to aid you in your work. They will come with great reluctance at first. Make your instructions clear and of good intent. As you strengthen your bond to Her, so her children will bond with you. Be forewarned, however. They do not restrain their childish pranks. A thing will go missing, keys will be lost, plants will be toppled, or any number of other mishaps can follow the calling of the earth creatures. They will not pass by the opportunity to laugh at humans. Be sure you deliberately state your rules about silly pranks. The firmer you are, the better they will behave. They do not have the grace of sylphs or salamanders, but their nighttime activities have taught them to move about quietly. And they are intelligent. Do not let their distance fool you. They know and see all.

Join me, Traveler. We will journey together through the Morrigan. It is worth your while to become acquainted with Her.

Crystals

Crystals and stones are some of the most beautiful gifts from the Mother. There are so many varieties, and so much knowledge can be gleaned from them. Older than time. Sage power and awesome energy. Getting to know crystals and their attributes will enhance your home, your work, and your spells. They will energize your environment and lend power to your rituals, deepening your intent. Their beauty is beyond words. As the Sun's or Moon's rays catch the stones laying in a bed of fine white sand by your window, you will delight in the prisms cast about your room. These are the Mother's true jewels. Not those which only a few can possess. Diamonds, emeralds, rubies—these are stones very few of us will acquire. They cannot be placed on our priority list. But crystals are affordable (free if you can find your own), plentiful and pleasing. The following are some of my favorites and their properties. Use them with only the bounds of your imagination to restrain you. Place them near plants for healing, in pouches for spell work, in baby's room for peace and growth, in the bathroom for meditative properties, near your doorways for protection or any other purposes which you feel comfortable with, so long as your intent remains pure. Enjoy the stones and crystals you gather. Your crystal garden will grow as you grow and gain power and energy. But do trust your feelings when choosing them. Make sure they feel right in your hands. If they do not, leave them be or try later. No piece of magical equipment you have should feel anything but entirely comfortable.

Amethyst

A stone of the most intense shades of purple to be found, the amethyst will draw your force in and wrap itself around you with a blanket of healing powers. It will aid you in your meditation and relaxation, and boost rituals and celebrations where ancient wisdom is sought.

Aventurine

The brilliant green of this crystal lends itself perfectly to prosperity and work-opportunity spells. Use its strong tangible forces to better your chances for job related help.

Bloodstone

A stone used for any healing pertaining to bleeding or the blood systems of our bodies. Prevents miscarriages, hemorrhages and severe bleeding, dangerous clotting, and lends power to positive surgical outcome.

Carnelian

This vivid orange-brown crystalline piece is one of the finest balancers available. It harmonizes an imbalanced household and soothes the decision making process if it is upsetting or stressful.

Clear Quartz

This stone strengthens the cords attaching you to the cosmos. It's power is that of tuning into the music of the spheres. It is a stone used commonly in jewelery, as wearing it will strengthen your ability to see the symbols and signals She sends us. Your eyes will be open.

Rose Quartz

Peace is the foundation of this rosy crystal. It's abundance makes it the ideal choice for beginner gardens. It relaxes the atmosphere in your home and tension is released.

Tiger Eye

A common stone, but a powerful one. The strength of this piece is its greatest attribute. It sends its user strength, courage, calm, and clearheadedness. It is a wonderful gift for students, academics, writers, etc. It is a thinking stone and should be placed at personal work spaces.

Tourmaline (Black)

This deep black stone protects you and your environment from negative influences and personalities. It should be used in purification rituals, in areas of your living or working environment which are not entirely comfortable; or a sickroom. It draws the negativity into itself and should be thoroughly cleansed after each use. This can be done by holding the stone under cool running water and then placing it on your altar for three days.

• • •

If you find that you use any stone a great deal, try to acquire more than one. This way, you can be using one of them and the other can be recharging on your altar or at your hearth.

Each type of stone has its powers. Research the many sources available for the listings of magical properties of stones and crystals. Many authors include lists in their books so sometimes you must dig. Interpretations of the stones and their uses can differ from writer to writer and you must try them out to find your comfortable use. Choose for yourself.

Stones can be kept on your altar or used on your hearth. Do be careful of your stones, they can chip or be scratched. If you are using them singly or as a grouping, place them on a piece of black or white velvet, cotton, or satin. Not only does this show off their beauty but it protects them from being knocked about.

A crystal garden is basically a dish lined with silica sand, and the stones are placed on top of the layer of sand. Silica sand can be purchased from any tropical fish or pet store. It is a powder-fine pure white sand which will not scratch or harm your stones. Be careful when using it. Watch your little ones as the sand is so fine, a heavy breath would blow it into their eyes. And it will stick to sticky little fingers and get rubbed into eyes. Children who touch the sand should wash their hands.

Place the stones in any pleasing pattern on the layer of sand. For your dish, use any wide-opening shallow dish which is esthetically pleasing. Many people like the shallow drainpans used for red clay pots. Plug the holes with paper and layer your sand. You will find that, over time, your stone gardens collect more than just stones. Things that have shown up in mine include seashells, bark, sprigs of plants, sticks, fossils, smoothed glass, a lock of my daughter's hair, and tiny notes. These are my treasures. I go through them regularly and put in my keepsake box any that can safely be stored. My gardens emit an energy which may be difficult to describe. But treasures gravitate toward it.

Do not place your stones on a bed of salt. This will eat away at the outer layers and will weaken them. If a small piece of one of your crystals should break off, use it in a spell, give it to a friend in need of its power, or grind it up to use in pouches. Don't throw it away. It has its power whether a small piece or large.

You will get to know the personalities of your stones. That is, of course, not meant literally. But each has its own unique vibratory energy, and you can and should work at recognizing these as individual. The simplest way to practice with both stones and herbs is to take each one in your hands and feel it. Really feel it—its temperature, texture, and vibration. Then blindfold yourself and pick each up one at a time. Try to distinguish the difference by vibration alone.

Gifts from the Mother

Different occasions in our lives call for a variety of gifts and small presents. Picking out just the right one is not always an easy task. If you enjoy giving gifts as much as I do, you want a personal and thoughtful item for the recipient. You want it to mean something and not just become another "garage sale" item. When I put together gifts, I want to get as much enjoyment out of preparing them as the person gets from receiving them.

There are many "wiccan" type gifts you can give. Individualized magical items make wonderful presents. They can be given singly or in groups arranged in a basket, pottery item, or pretty container. But each will be empowered with a specific quality that will aid or enhance the life of the person you give it to.

Pouches are a very individualized item. They can be made from any material you wish. I tend to use felt, because it can be purchased reasonably and in a wide range of colors, and I am able to completely custom design my gifts. Births, showers, birthdays, anniversaries and any other occasions—pouches can be created for potent blessings, healing, congratulations, etc. Choosing the right stone, herb, token, and words to put in the pouches makes use of your imagination and research skills.

Combine pouches with an assortment or individual candles and add a small bundle of an appropriate herb. A small blend of bath herbs and some incense makes a unique and personalized gift. Decorate the basket with ribbons or plants. Add seashells if representation of the water element is called for, such as a birth.

For occasions of love such as marriages, anniversaries, or engagements, amethyst would be my first choice. It has the ability to enhance ancient wisdom for the user. It gives glimpses into past relationships with the user's beloved. It deepens the ritual and emotions of the occasion. Its pale purple is lovely but nothing is quite so beautiful as the deep, deep purple variety. Gazing into the heart of these stones, one can see all time at once. The importance of seizing the moment is clear. You become very aware that love knows no boundaries in time.

For births, christenings, and wiccanings, rose quartz is a perfect gift addition. Because of its soothing affects, this beautiful stone can be tucked up on a shelf in baby's room and keep the atmosphere of the nursery calm and peaceful. It has a wonderful effect on colicky babies and helps with parents' patience.

In the case of funerals or wakes, quietly give a smoky quartz to family members. This stone will bring them the peace they need, and at the same time, will enable them to move forward. Unanswerable questions will be reconciled by the spirit and loved ones will realize that life does go on.

Finding just the right stone as a gift is not as complicated as one might think. If you are clear in your mind that you wish to give a gift of the Mother, one will come to you. Watch for the circumstances because they will make themselves known. This holds true in most aspects of life. When you have needed something, it has usually been there. I mean really needed something. It may not always have come in the way you would have wanted or expected, but things have a way of working out.

When choosing stones, hold them in your hands and picture the person to whom they are going. If a connection is made, you will feel peaceful with that choice. If you perceive any negativity at all when you envision the person and stone together, choose another or try later. The feeling should be just right. Don't worry about not recognizing it. You will. Just relax when you hold the stone and breathe deeply. Let it sit in the palm of your receptive hand and feel it's vibratory energy. Let this energy merge with your own as you keep a firm picture of the person in your mind. Trust your own instincts.

Earth on Your Altar

Aside from the wonderful and powerful varieties of stone that you can use in ritual, at your altar, around your home and near your hearth, there are many other representations of the earth element that you can use.

Sand, salt, earth, herbs, live plants, twigs/sticks, bundles of wheat and pebbles are all clear representatives of our great Mother. These things can be found, given to you as a gift, purchased yourself, or made by you or a friend. As with stones and many other magical things, these representations have a habit of popping up. Just when you need that element strengthened or your awareness is drifting, they come into your life.

A small container of salt should grace a formal altar at all times. This is a regular item used in most rituals or spell-workings. But many informal, small, or casual altars or hearths do not need salt specifically. You must be careful what container you choose to put it in, as salt will eat away at many materials. During some rituals, I add a pinch of salt to the water in my chalice and I am very careful about rinsing it out after the ceremony. My chalice is pewter and the salt can leave nasty erosion in metals and raw pottery. Better to use another container or another representation.

The very dark potting soil available at most garden centers makes a lovely earth symbol. It not only feels soft and fine in the hands, it smells of the Morrigan, that wonderful earthy, damp smell. Only a pinch is needed for most spells or rituals. You can add that spelled pinch to wax tokens, pouches, or altarspace. Use your imagination. You will know what feels right.

Herbs, of course, are a gift from the mother. I'm sure you can tell that I use them a great deal in my work, for my family, magically and medicinally. They are as varied as stones, and I find that I have so many to choose from. Often times, the properties of both stones and herbs overlap. That is to say, many have similar or the same qualities. Use the ones you like the best. There is nothing wrong with not liking something. Just because you are wiccan does not mean you are obligated to like all elemental gifts. I am not particularly fond of either curry or anise seed. But I can find these qualities in other herbs and spices.

Perhaps now would be a good time to touch on one of the more unique representations of the earth element. I mentioned earlier that a bundle of wheat on your altar is a solid earth symbol. Of course, for celebrations such as the Autumnal Equinox and Samhain, a bundle of wheat or grain shows thanks for bountiful harvests at this time. These are our celebrations of life and the gifts of food she provides us with.

But at any other times of the year, these same symbols stand out as being truly representative of the planet on which we make our home. If you live in the city and do not have any access to "country" items, often small groceries and specialty ethnic stores sell bundles of sage, dill, and other herbs. Or ask a friend with a garden to keep a bundle for you. But these bundles do not have to be grains or herbs. A bundle of any plant variety will do. Back lane weeds will do the job, too. If your elemental representations have a part in your work or ritual, then you must pick the right ones for the work. But if the main function of these items is to represent a particular element, then their magical properties stands separate from that task.

When I am developing a spell or work that needs doing, I go through a list of questions to organize my project. Perhaps my questions will help people who are just learning to put together spells. You don't have to specifically follow a "recipe" from a book. I stress in my writing that you should use your feelings, imagination, and intuition for your work. Break free of the idea that you must do certain things a certain way. The freedom of the Craft is precisely why I was attracted to it. It does not have doctrines and rules. So long as your intent is good and kind, you are free to do your work with anything and in any way. Here are the things which I ask myself:

1) What is the specific intent of this work? Spellwork can be categorized in three basic ways—love, money or healing. Love incorporates any work which has to do with interpersonal relationships, bonding, or family. Money encompasses prosperity, job, career advancement, and success in projects or ventures. Healing, of course, covers all aspects of medicinal work, tension relief, blessings, and work dealing with the human spirit.

2) What words do I wish to use for this work? Spells should be written precisely and succinctly. You should give great thought to this aspect of working. Use an economy of words and say exactly what you mean. Watch the wording because a misstated spell can go awry.

3) What herbs or stones would best suit my purpose? This stage needs research. Unless you are well versed in the magical properties of the herbs and stones, you should look them up to be sure.

4) What color would empower my work? You will find a color chart in Appendix 2 and you can choose a color for your candles, stones, or garb that would work best.

5) What time of day or month would create more power for my work? In chapter 7, I discuss times of day, month, and year. But you must, again, research and choose the best times for you.

6) What elements do I need represented according to the work I am doing? You will have to answer this for yourself.

7) Will this work harm anyone? This is the most important question of all. Examine your purpose, intent, and goal. If it will cause anyone any distress or negativity, DO NOT DO IT.

Once you have answered these questions, you will have a clear guide as to what you will need for the work you want to do. Choose your magical items, time, and place. Learn to trust your instincts. Put together your spells using the knowledge you have gleaned so far in your Craft life. As you accumulate more knowledge, you will find your choices increase and your work is enhanced. But begin with what you know already.

As you do your work, be secure in the knowledge that we all started out as beginners. Often, new Witches will feel amateurish and awkward. But this is normal when we start on any new path. One cannot know all there is to know. We must learn as everyone else has had to. And you can be sure that you will never know everything there is to know about the Craft. There are so many differing opinions, suggestions and instructions, that your only choice is to listen to your intuition. I am happy practicing the Craft as I have, putting together the work I do with my own knowledge and feeling. I read any book I can get my hands on and incorporate what I read into the storehouse of knowledge I already have. Then I sift through it to use what is comfortable to me. I'm sure I will get some letters telling me that there are strict rules, initiations, and practices that MUST be adhered to. But I disagree. The Craft is freedom. I have been through the degrees of initiation, but even without them, I would be a witch. I love the fact that we have so much literature and information to glean our practices from.

My home and family, writing career, and the Craft are all a part of me. I develop new spells, herbal works, pot-pourris and aesthetic practices all the time. I do what is comfortable and practical. You must not let someone tell you that you are wrong if you know your work to be accurate and of good intent. Know in your heart that you are celebrating the Gods and your Craft work will reflect that. If someone tries to make you feel less of a witch because you don't follow particular paths, you should seriously question their motives. I have met a few in the Craft who feel that one tradition is better or more powerful than another. But this is not the case. Practice YOUR Craft and enjoy your work.

Many of the letters I receive from readers have shown me clearly that there are many of you out there who really are Craft to your very souls. Your warm wishes and nice comments about the Craft and my work have made it all worth while. I now regularly correspond with many of you. Your integrity and positive feelings come through in your letters.

The Earth and All She Gives

This chapter is about earth and the gifts that are given into our care for our use. And perhaps, there is no better place in this book to talk about environmental practices than in a section discussing Her gifts and attributes.

As pagans, we must constantly be aware of our behavior toward the environment. We must develop and maintain positive awareness of just what our planet is about and how we can preserve and care for it. We have not treated her very well and she is responding.

If we were to get into a time machine and travel back two hundred years, there is a good chance that we would have a great deal of difficulty breathing when we stepped out. The air we breathe today is so full of pollutants and gases that our systems and lungs have developed some immunity to them. We have evolutionarily adapted to the violent changes in our planet's true nature. That is sad. Instead of enjoying what is given to us, we, as a species, have taken advantage of what is here for us.

Try to contemplate this on a smaller scale and it will become much clearer. Suppose that someone has given you a new home.

Free and clear of debt, you move into your new environment and settle in. Now try to picture yourself never vacuuming, dusting, or washing it. Never picking up garbage or sweeping floors. Never cleaning your bathroom or changing your bed linens. What a horrible thought! And I don't know anyone that could possibly be content to live in this manner. Not only would your environment get unbearable, but you would not treat so great a gift in this manner. But what is the difference between this fictional house and the Earth?

We must now work together to bring Her back to life and repair the damage that has been done. So many people think that it is not their responsibility. Especially those who are over forty. I have heard so many say that the polluting factories and practices were developed and built before they were born. But that does not change the fact that we must fix it. Some of these practices were around before I was born. It would be very easy to blame the older generation, to lay the responsibility at their feet. But this is not how things work. We are all brothers and sisters. We must pull together. Blame is a wasted emotion. It serves no useful purpose at all. It merely serves to alleviate guilt. But to feel a little guilt in this circumstance would be very appropriate.

Many people seem to think that the little things won't count. But they do. Very much. I was speaking to someone about individual recycling and reuse. I was told that large corporations and-high-volume polluters were doing little or nothing to repair global damage, so what could our little contribution make? If everyone would get into the habit of recycling, reducing, and reusing, it would make a grand difference. Those of us who live environmentally aware make a difference. Being aware means that we can teach the children and generations to come that these practices are necessary. Children learn by example.

7

Nights and Days

ow that I have discussed the elements and their fundamental powers and significance, I would like to devote some space to the magic and power of the Moon, woman-spirit, nights and days, pregnancy and childbirth, and the seasonal celebrations. Much of this is common knowledge. Much of this is my own philosophy.

Magic is a very individual thing. For some it means slight-of-hand/illusionary stage entertainment. But for us, magic is all around us and in us. It starts at our core and ends with the limits our imagination set on it. It is a part of our everyday existence, our everyday awareness of the magic in life. We need to be able to recognize the wondrous magical properties we have at our fingertips.

For me, the magic in my life comes from within me, from my surroundings, from my loved ones, and from the phases of the Moon and the seasonal powers. I draw from all that I can. I search out the places where magic may linger. I use what is available and am constantly striving to develop new ways to celebrate my Crafthood.

I enjoy being a pagan. I need to practice as a witch. This is a very fundamental need in me. I could not turn my back on the Craft. As I go through my day, I find myself working magic often. Much of it is so subtle and unplanned that it is only after I have finished that I realize what I have done. Many of my works I do for family and friends. But much of it is as inconspicuous as having a cup of tea. Earlier I mentioned that when I light a candle or brew a cup of tea, I do not waste these motions. If I am brewing mint tea, for example, I will deliberately picture a person in my life who needs the prosperity and protection of that herb. I then drink the tea with a specific purpose. The same is true when lighting a candle. Don't waste that golden opportunity to use the flame to enhance someone's world. Each of these practices may be common and almost automatic but don't let the chance for magic pass.

Magic will be available even for those who don't use it. Being wiccan is using what is available and grasping the power. Some witches are "Sunday" witches, going to Sabbats, working at Esbats, but not bringing the "stuff" of the universe into their lives. Keeping in touch is what daily hearth-magic is about. Without it, I would be lost. I need the power that comes from using my knowledge. Just as with anything, magic gets stronger, easier, and more understood with use. A tale is only a tale with the telling. Magic is only truly magic with the using. The more magic you use in your daily life, the more positive energy is generated. And all of us can use more positivity in our live. So use it! Enjoy it! Make your magic a part of your life and you will be stronger for it.

Stages of the Goddess

Women go through three stages in their lives, if they have an average lifespan and if they make the full transition from one stage to another. Some stop at one and remain there with the wisdom that this stage brings. Others journey through all three, and at the end of their lives, their eyes glisten with the wisdom of the Crone.

Men experience these phases, too, but in a different way. They must meet each milestone with the *Anima* (the female aspect within each man) primed, but society does not necessarily afford them the opportunity to explore outwardly these aspects.

In the 90s, men are respected for raising children and being more in touch with the family. House-husbandry is not to be ridiculed any longer. Men are free to cry, feel pain, and love, if they allow themselves to do so. Thank the gods, it is about time. Men deserve the option of choosing to be open and frank.

The Maiden aspect of the Goddess is one of gaiety, impulsiveness, purity of soul, and animation. If a woman has made a smooth transition from the Maiden to the Mother, she will find herself pondering her youth now and then, but knowing and being aware of the lessons and experience she gleaned from her past. She will know herself clearly. She will start to correct some of her self-defeating habits and behaviors. She will know that this takes time and that she cannot "become" without awareness of having "been." She will be more tolerant of herself and others and the interactions between.

A woman *does not* automatically move to the Mother stage at the birth of a child. Many women experience frustration and anxiety at being mothers. They have not finished in the Maiden stage and are still dependent on characteristics present in that stage: over-indulgence, abuse of pleasurable habits, lack of patience. This may sound rather harsh but we are humans, guilty of many faults and downfalls. The trick is becoming aware of these childlike traits, be they negative or positive, and adjusting them to the growth in our lives.

The Mother stage can be a difficult transition. A woman can be reluctant to let go the ways of her youth. A woman learns to integrate positive habits acquired in youth with the maturation and creativity of the Mother stage. The transition is accompanied by the ability to take life and see it as a ladder. Each rung of the ladder opens our eyes a little wider. If we use energy to re-step a rung, we will be lacking for energy to move upward on that ladder.

The Crone stands solitary and unbending. She *knows* what is necessary. She has taken the lessons in and sees clearly the ways in which she grew within or denied herself knowledge. She knows what must be done on the road ahead. She has readied herself for the journey.

We all carry habits borrowed from previous stages. Nervous habits, fears, and self-defeating modes of behavior all contribute to the slowing of inner growth. Women let go of "previous-stage" behavior in order to put their environment at ease, lessening the tension of the growth process. Women do not have to let go of traits from previous stages but must learn to incorporate new ones so that each stage is enhanced. Each stage of life allows us to "fine-tune" traits learned from former stages. Women can mourn the past, but must learn to let go of negativity. The greatest responsibility we have is to be as happy as we can be. If we are not happy with our own growth and change, we cannot possibly expect ourselves to help others. We cannot be all that we can be without living through and learning what each of our Goddess stages offers.

Moon Phases

The Moon's three phases are expressed by Wiccans as the phases of the Goddess. The Waxing Moon is the Goddess in her Maiden stage, the Full Moon is the Mother ripe with life and the Waning Moon gives us the Goddess in her Crone stage, the stage of wisdom.

Each night that the moon is visible, I try to say hello. I gaze up at her and know where my power comes from. I see her new slivered form, or her full belly, or I see her not at all. But no matter what phase she is in, she is the Lady and she grants me power.

Women and men physiologically relate to the lunar phases. Every living creature and plant reacts to this orb's influence, in mood, emotion, and behavior. Ask any police personnel, emergency room staff, or mental health professional. All have seen the effects of the moon's phases on human beings. The legends and fears of Full Moon lunacy are not without basis. The tides are programmed by the movement and phases of the moon, as well. But nothing is quite so apparent to lunar life as the menstrual cycle of a woman. She has the Goddess within her and bleeding and childbirth are all part of a grand design with the moon at the helm.

I have talked at great length to women friends and family members about their cycles, moods, and emotions. Most agree that the twenty-eight day cycle which dictates bleeding (or lack of it in the case of pregnancy) has a direct effect on what they feel, wear, and do.

During the waxing phase of the Lady, I tend to be very energetic and somewhat colorful. My favorite color is usually black, but during this phase, I brighten my wardrobe with splashes of color from scarves, jewelery or makeup. When She is in her Mother stages, I wear more subdued colors, and at the dark of the moon you will find me in black. I noticed this pattern many years ago. It's not a regimen that I consciously keep; it's dictated by the emission of power and energy from Lady Moon. Few women are aware of their dress or behavior as it relates to the moon. I keep journals and it helps me track my movements and moods at different times during the lunar month. Unless a woman is very aware of herself and the times of month, she will not notice these subtle changes. Wiccan women tend to be more aware of which phase the moon is in at any given time.

My work is a direct reflection of these phases, too. During the Waxing Moon, I do work for others. It is powerful and emits great energy. With onset of the Full Moon, my work is bold and full. It is more immediately centered in me and directly around me. During the dark of the moon, if work is necessary, I tend to keep focused on my environment. But during this phase, I am very aware of my inner self and the "self" that needs to learn and grow. I find this a good phase for any study which I have embarked upon. My mental and emotional capacities are wide open and hungry for more wisdom. Keeping a journal is a wonderful way to track our needs and work, and every woman should keep one.

Magic's essence changes with the seasonal and lunar wheels. Our work will change and the outcome of our magic and spells has a direct effect on upon our emotional and spiritual well-being. Because the energy we use during spells or ritual is coming from us via a circuitous route through the heavens, we must remain aware of the changes these cycles create in us and about us. If we are not aware, we are only getting benefit of half of the power available. So, to strengthen our work and ourselves, we must be aware. Watch for the changes in the night sky and see the turning of the seasonal wheel. Become attuned to the unique differences that the lunar month holds.

Most calendars have the moon's phases marked on them. There are a few wonderful pagan calendar books available as well. These books list lunar phases, seasonal celebrations, and ethnic festivals. Books of this kind are needed for beginners on this path. Without being aware, you are cheating yourself and your work of the power that this awareness brings. Keep current on the cyclical nature of the universe and all it holds. The ancients knew what to look for and used these signs as a guidepost to their religious celebrations and magical deeds.

One evening years ago, I heard a little poem on the sit-com Night Court. It went something like this:

Hey diddle, diddle, The cat and the fiddle,
is a lie like all the best.
The astronauts killed the man in the moon,
growing up took care of the rest.

We do not have to let the romance go! We can keep the magical power of the moon and the heavens. Don't let your hold slip. Just because we know what the surface of the moon looks like or that there are footprints on the moon, doesn't mean that we have to let go of our dreams and magical fantasies. I can use technology all day (writing on a computer, for example) and gaze at the night sky with an ancient's eyes. I must. I would wither and die without seeing the heavens. The Apollo crew found no man or woman in the moon, but these old phrases and fables came from the hearts and souls of those who had no better way of describing what they experienced.

Nights and Days

Just as the moon is a direct reflection of the phases of the Goddess, so, too, is the twenty-four hour period which we call "day." The waxing of a day is the time between dawn and noon, the full of a day is from noon until dusk, and the waning or dark of the day is from dusk until dawn. Your magic will benefit from knowing this correlation to the lunar cycles. The emotion and energy used at these various times corresponds to the moods and changes described earlier.

One thing that most human beings seem to miss is that everything in our world works on a microcosmic/macrocosmic scale. As above, so below. Each cell in our bodies works with the same energy as each star in the sky. What happens in the microscopic world also happens in the macroscopic universe. The heavenly bodies (planets, stars, suns, moons) are all just cells in the body of the Goddess. We are Her nerve endings in this world. We feel for her, we taste, smell, and touch for her. We are her communication links. From the tiniest creature or plant, to the largest star or planet, all life works from the same source of power. This is something we must remember when using magic.

Pregnancy and Childbirth

In our world of miracles and magic, there is nothing so powerful or magical as the creation of a new being. Nothing! This is not to say that one must experience childbirth to feel this. Men and women together create life. Regardless of a woman's ability or lack of ability to give birth, the power remains the same. Men are a necessary part of this process and together we carry on our species on this planet. Without one or the other we would be lost. Even women who are unable to bear children should recognize their nurturing qualities and realize that these qualities are a gift we must use. There are children in this world who need the love and nurturing that we can give them. And as fellow human beings, we are responsible for each and every one. We must take care of babies. They are her babies and they deserve the best our time, talents, and money have to offer. And each of us has an obligation to help in whatever capacity we can. Children do not deserve to be without food or adequate shelter and clothing.

During pregnancy, a woman's "visible" monthly lunar cycle is no longer there. So she must pay even closer attention to the ways and moods of her month. These, of course, are amplified by the river of hormones rushing through her. Just ask anyone who has been through a pregnancy. Moods are unpredictable and irrational. The greatest obsticle we face is that we know this, but we are powerless to do anything about it. We consume all the right foods, we sleep as much as our time allows and we excersise and walk when we can. But still those hormones rage on. This is not to imply that all pregnant women are impossible to live with. On the contrary, we are often joyous and happy, but our bodies are coping with a myriad of changes and our energy is drained in ways we could not imagine.

During my recent pregnancy, I lost complete use of my receptive abilities. I could not get a link going with my intuition. And I felt helpless. It was as if one of my fundimental senses had abandoned me. And indeed it had. The energy I used for empathic work was now being rerouted to the baby to aid its development. It took awhile to get accustomed to this void sensation, and I continued my magical work with some slight modifications. The following is a continuous spell I used to substitute for my loss of intuitive power:

> Mauve candle;
> Raspberry leaves;
> A pinch of hair (my own).

The mauve candle was used because any shade of purple is used for intuitive or psychic work. Raspberry leaves are very much the herb for pregnancy because one of its finer aspects is that of attunment. A tiny portion of my hair was the key to establishing a link between the cosmos and myself.

The words that I used were tailored to my personal search for connection. The important part of this spell is the wax token I made from the mauve wax, the raspberry, my hair and the ashes from my spell. I carried this with me most of my pregnancy. Despite my loss of intuitive powers, I knew that this spell would warn me if a situation arose in which those powers would normally kick into high gear. The most annoying aspect of my loss was the ability to tune into another person's mood and emotions. The majority of my power was devoted to the life growing inside of me. But there are always ways to compensate for the loss of one sense.

Some women I have talked to have felt an increase in their intuitive senses, but this is rare. When a woman is pregnant, she is doing one job and one job only. Her entire being is devoted to this function. Yes, she can carry on her mundane life, work, and necessary tasks, but the magical part of her being is busy dividing cells, forming features, and nourishing the tiny life in her belly. The Goddess created a perfect machine when she created us. This miracle we call birth is indeed just that. It is the finest example of perfection available.

Just as a person who loses one of their five senses increases the strength of the others, so, too, with the magical senses. I found my powers of transmission greater. The ability to transmit thought and energy became strong and sure. I could do work for others with little effort. My spells for healing and other's needs were potent and powerful.

When pregnant, a witch will find herself pulled to the natural and magical forces in the universe. Our focus is on health and the wonderful bounty of the Goddess. As our bellies grow, so do we. We grow with the light of her in our eyes. We are drawn to things which tell this tale—herbs, plants, our homes, our families, and ourselves. Our energy is nurture-based. We are creators. Building this little being is the most incredible task we will ever undertake.

Once Hannah was born, I found that my powers of intuition returned. Almost immediately! How surprised I was in the birthing room when the emotions of those around me crept in with feeling and blended with mine. And this mist of energy washed over me like a tidal wave. Suddenly I could sense again. There were the auras of all those around me. Including this little girl who's dependency on me alone had suddenly changed. I no longer had to nourish her from inside of me. She was there to touch, and smell, and care for, and love. But "I" had returned and that too, felt wonderful—a bit disconcerting for a moment, but wonderful.

With magic as an aid, pregnancy is a magnificent state. We are given just enough time to adjust to the idea of caring for a helpless human being. We grow with the baby and are reborn with it. Revel in this continuance of our species, for it is a miracle. Enjoy the changes and life-giving powers of growing round with child. You will blossom and glow. She feels through you and will endow you with gifts beyond your comprehension if only you are open to them. Let your magic run free and it will bless you with power.

There are many magical ways in which a partner can help to make a pregnancy happy and ease the burden of changes in a woman's body. Spells of relaxation and calm are always a plus when one is going through such tremendous shifts in power. Help her with her intuition. Become her sense for a time. Watch over her and nurture her. She is busy nurturing the babe inside. She will need kindness, compassion, empathy, and love. Hold her, love her and be patient with her. She needs you now more than ever. Let her cry on your shoulder for she will cry. Let her lay in your arms and soak up the love you have for her. Keep her as content as possible for she is busy. Very, very busy. Carrying a baby is a big job and the more you can help her to enjoy this time in her life, the more calm and healthy your baby will be. Babies are aware of their mothers' moods, emotions, and stresses. Talk to the little one together. Play music for it. Rub her belly. All these things can be sensed by the child. It will bond with it's nurturers and feel secure.

Even the timing surrounding a child's birth is an amazing display of symbols and the weave of life's fabric. My baby was born exactly nine months to the day of my mother's passing and became my Beltane babe. I was given a calendar of daily sayings for Yule when I was carrying her. On Christmas Eve, I was glancing through these sayings and one caught my eye. It said— "Wisdom doesn't come from study. Knowledge does. Wisdom comes from showing up for life." This was the saying for April 27th. My baby was due April 30th. Due to a bout of flu, she came into this world on April 27th. I will keep that page forever. I somehow knew that this particular day's blurb was important and kept it aside from Yule on. Imagine my wonder when I realized just how important that day was.

Keep your eyes open for the messages she sends you. Often in our lives, we are too busy to be aware of the subtle signs that are ours to see. Know that with childbirth, as with other important events or circumstance in our lives, we are given signs and hints. But we must be open and receptive to them.

Before a woman is due to deliver, she should be mentally, emotionally, and psychically preparing herself for this wonderful process. If she is healthy, and the pregnancy is going well, raspberry leaf tea is a potent aid in the upcoming labor experience. Many women have used this herb as a supplement to their daily intake of food and liquid. Its properties include easing the labor pain, reducing swelling of the limbs, and refreshing the bladder. Any medicinal use of an herb should be thoroughly researched before use, and a soon-to-be-mom should feel comfortable with using "alternative" medicines. Some people do not feel safe with anything outside the allopathic medical community's view of medicine, and many pregnant women feel doubly so at this time in their lives. By talking to their physician and one or two herbalists, as well as doing detailed reading with regard to a particular herb, many women are willing to use natural aids to the birth process.

Throughout a pregnancy, women can practice and become proficient in the art of self-meditation and self-hypnosis. The more relaxed you can become and the more focused you are during this process, the smoother and more enjoyable it will be. And believe me, it can truly be one of the greatest times in your life!

Spells for relaxation and preparation can have very beneficial effects. A partner can always help with work of this kind. Spelling for your partner will help to link with the mother and baby. The greater the feeling of connectedness, the stronger the bonding becomes. For spells of relaxation and meditation, use stones such as amethyst, bloodstone and rose quartz, combined with lemon balm or cinnamon. Choose your words carefully and use the Full Moon phase. This phase is the most potent for work of this kind. Your work can incorporate anything that you feel comfortable with.

Take long walks. Unless you are suffering severe swelling in your legs and ankles, walking will help your circulation and muscles. Always rest with your feet up after walks, if possible. Enjoy the power of the elements. Breathe deeply of the air, drink in the warming rays of the sun, feel the moisture in all that grows around you, and receive the power of the earth path you walk. Absorb the energies that are being given for your benefit. They are continuously being replenished so you cannot use them up. Don't be afraid to pull in all that you can.

Pathwork to the Crone

On the spiral that is life, within the circle, we meet her again and again. Once each lunar cycle and after the Samhain Sabbat. In her lunar aspect she is the way to dark, earth magic. She is the giver of power, the sage for the Self. She enables us to do work which is from or away from the Self. Work which sends. She is the time of power that allows us to see deeper into the essence that is the moon.

In her Wheel aspect, the Crone is the source of wisdom. She alone will decide if we are ready. She, of course, is this aspect, but buried deep within the Self. She is a reflection of wisdom illusive yet still there to be used.

Come meet with her. Know her for all that she is and all that she knows. When you meet her, embrace her, for you will be embracing yourself. She will cause you to be aware. She knows that awareness is wisdom. This is her essence, her blood.

Through dark, deep forests the Crone waits. Bent over her cane, the handle worn smooth from an eternity of rubbing. Her dark hood hides all. Look carefully at the hand which pushes back the hood. All children, her hand has touched the head of each. Soothed the brow of the lost child. Rubbed the belly of the laboring woman. Held the hand of each dying elder. Held as rebirth awaits.

She pushes away material which shades her eyes, the eyes that have seen eternal births and deaths. Look deeply into them. Know them, for they know you. Let them reflect the simple matters for these bring with them awareness. Look closely at her face. Gaze deeply into the lines of experience which grace her brow. An eternity of truths are etched deep in each and every groove. Her face has seen all that has been and all that will be. It can be fierce and kind, harsh and gentle, old and young. Get to know her, and she will show herself to you more fully. She will allow you the awareness you seek.

She is the dark mother. She is the keeper of the path to rebirth. She is the giver of knowledge through darkness, emerging into the light of spring. Take her hand and hold it tightly. Through touch does she give. She speaks not, for words are inadequate. Feel the essence of all that is known pass from her fingertips to your own. Pull the power into your Greater Self. Experience the simples. The more you can draw from her, the closer she is to her own rebirth. She must give to you to survive. She and you are one. You must give to yourself to survive. She will show you the way. She will smile at you with her eyes. She knows you are receptive to what she has to give. Memorize that face. You will know it many times, until one day you see it in the mirror. And wisdom will be yours.

The Witch's Wheel

I would like first to talk about the Lesser Sabbats. The reason being that these festival times of the Wheel are perhaps, the least understood. Each of the Greater Sabbats has a folk energy. Its pagan roots have their essence in lore and belief of fable. But the Lessers have only their position on the Wheel as their foundation for celebrations.

The Vernal Equinox: March 21st is the time of the wheel to fully incorporate the newness of Spring, and its atmosphere of rebirth, into your home and hearth. Each year we face the seasons as markers for our lives. Remember the microcosmic/macrocosmic principle. The old saying "in the spring/summer/autumn of his years" refers to the seasons of our lives. Each season has its aspects to rejoice. The Spring Equinox is a time to celebrate the newness of life. The seedlings and babies abound. New growth everywhere. Promise fills our world. So much is fresh and pure— the air, the earth, the fields, and springs. Everything sheds its dark coat of winter and bursts into the light of the new sun.

Bring this stop on the Wheel into your home by filling it with whatever signs of new life you can find. Eggs are extreme- ly popular this time of the year. Decorate them, hollow them, dis- play them and eat them. They are a representation of all that is new birth. We rediscover ourselves after the long, dark winter. We peek from our blankets of hermitism and are ready to face the prospects of a whole new start.

Colors for the Vernal Equinox usually range through the pas- tel shades of green, yellow, and violet. These shades can be rep- resented throughout your home by making very simple changes. The minor changes I make at this time of year contribute to not only my recognition of the turning of the wheel, but also to my state of mind. During the long winter I tend to use woven place- mats and couch covers, while in the spring I bring out the linen or cotton ones. I buy small sprays of fresh flowers. I burn more brightly colored candles and I get rid of stale old bunches of winter herbs. My supermarket carries a small variety of fresh herbs so I replenish some stock. I transplant my house plants, clean out and redo my crystal gardens, and reorganize my hearth places. My magical equipment gets a thorough scrubbing out and sorting. There are psychological purposes behind the idea of "spring cleaning." We must shake out the cobwebs and open our eyes. During the winter we have been busy learning, researching, writing, or contemplating. Winter is a wonderful time for that kind of inner growth, but Spring is the time to throw open windows in both your house and your mind.

The Summer Solstice: June 21st and 22nd brings with it a time of leisure and relaxation. Even if you must work each day or deal with mundane problems and responsibilities, you must strive to find the time you require during this season. Eat of the wonderful summer harvests that the greengrocer has to offer. Make and invent new summer salads, juices and ice teas. Use lots of water during this season if possible (not of course, if your area is restricted in water consumption). But you can also make use of the water element by filling a small pool and splashing in it. Summer is a time for childlike play and water is very hard to resist on a hot afternoon. We can all revert to childhood when handed a squirtgun. Have fun, eat well, and be happy!

The Autumnal Equinox: September 21st is the time of the Wheel for preparation. We can ring in the season by canning, freezing, and enjoying the bounty of the fall harvest. Feasts of root vegetables, squash, and sweet potatoes combine with roasts spiced with sage (for those who eat meat). Fall aromas are everywhere. Collect the fresh fall herbs, bundle them and hang them in your kitchen. The pleasant earthy scents will freshen that room for the long months ahead. Plenty of grain displays, Indian corn, and popped corn adorn the hearth. Munch on the popped corn. Without butter, this makes a low cal snack for those who must watch their weight in the winter. Decorate with the fall colors of gold, red, brown, dark green, and orange. Iron leaves between sheets of waxed paper like you did as a child. Do this with your

children. They can hang them in their rooms or make a collage.
Fill your house with the harvest reminders. This is a time of
thanksgiving, a time for rejoicing for the plentiful growing season. Being truly grateful for all that we have and how blessed we
are!

The Winter Solstice: December 21st and 22nd is often celebrat-
ed with Christmas, but my suggestion to you would be to keep
Yule and Christmas somewhat separate. If you celebrate both,
aspects of each can be combined with the other to enhance both
days, but Yule has very specific focuses for those of us who recognize this wonderful time.

Yule is a time to use greens and golds, silver, red, and white.
It is a celebration of the learning months ahead. It ushers in the
darker days of winter and relaxes us for the lessons of thought
which we have yet to learn. We are welcoming the colder season.
Holly and pine are my two favorite scents for the solstice, and
pine-tar burned on a coal fills the house with holiday atmosphere.

Light plenty of candles, use your hearth is you have one,
burn sweet smelling logs, decorate with pine cones and nuts. And
be sure to leave plenty of crusts for the birds.

The Greater Sabbats

Imolg: February 2nd is a celebration of the very first stirrings of
life. Not the process of birth, but the process of creation, of two
cells combining and dividing, of life on the cellular level, of the
initial yearnings for the light of spring. To recognize and acknowl-
edge this celebration, one can decorate with darker tones and
heavier scents. Use cinnamon as a foundation for incenses and
offerings, as this herb represents creation and life. Use this festival time for reflection of beginnings and memories of innocence.
Refresh yourself for the warmth of the seasons to come. Use baths
scented with coriander and lavender to renew your skin.

Beltane: April 30th is the festival for celebrating the process of the hunt, mating, partnering, and birth. Let all who feast do so with thanks for our cyclical nature. Both on the microcosmic and macrocosmic level, life is renewing and replenishing itself. Everything is bursting forth with freshness and energy. The process of growth is at its peak for birth. See Spring spiral toward full bounty and harvest.

In Beltane lore, the Maiden of the coven or village would hunt the King-stag (lover to the maiden) to mate with him and form a partnership. The Maiden fervently wished to become pregnant with a Beltane babe. This would signify to the village that the harvests for the coming Summer and Fall would be plentiful. The stag would wear horns and a stag's pelt thrown over his shoulders. This re-enactment of the Goddess' hunt for her Forest God allowed the ancients—and allows contemporary pagans—to "touch" the forest and praise the glorious life growing around them.

Lughnasadh: July 31st-August 1st is a celebration of the Sun God and the light, warmth, and life we derive from this magnificent heavenly source. All of life is at its peak of perfection. Following this time, plants begin to go to seed, harvests begin in earnest and every activity gears toward the coming months of work and storage. Use plenty of green, blue, and yellow. Burn dill, basil, and thyme if you can. Harvesting these herbs is a wonderful feeling and all can be grown indoors for those who do not have a garden. Use agates in your magical work. Agates are great stones for the generation of energy. And for the preparations we all must make for Fall and Winter, more energy is always a "hot commodity."

Fill your celebrations with representations of the fire element and the sun's warmth. Try midday rituals. Many witches do not conduct rituals until after the sun sets. But a midday ritual gives you the opportunity to feel the sun as you do your work. Give the early morning a chance to brighten your work, too. Have a cup of ritual tea in the first hours of day. Breathe deeply by the window or outdoors. This is a fresh and clean time of day and you will enjoy taking advantage of it's many calming aspects. Try different times to see which you like.

Samhain: October 31st is the Witches' New Year. We celebrate the death of all that carried us through the year and provided so much for the dark months ahead. It is a celebration of the final harvests and the cessation of work in the fields.

Samhain celebrates the lives of those who have gone before us. We leave candles in the windows and carve jack-o-lanterns to scare away the mischievous spirits. Many pagans set an extra place at their feasts to feed the returning dead. This particular time of year provides for the thinnest veil between our worlds and the dead can walk freely in ours. Most of today's Halloween decorations derive from the ancient pagan celebrations for the close of the year.

Use Fall colors in your celebrations. Harvest vegetables and meats, with specific emphasis on grain products, should fill your feast table. Use apple as your primary scent for this season. Chop it and let it dry on your windowsills and in pot-pourris. Soak the chopped pieces in a bit of vinegar for an hour or two before adding to your scent mixtures, as this helps stop any rot that might form. Or dry pieces and then burn them in your ritual cauldron or on a coal.

I prefer to leave my house and circle rather dark at this time of year. I enjoy the darkness as a prelude to the indoor, learning months of winter, an introduction of sorts. Let the atmosphere of your home permeate your being. Usher in the coming Winter with celebration and mystery.

THE WHEEL

Imolg ushers in the first hint of spring
    and life begins to breath,
The festivals burst with hope and farewell
    to winter's quiet ease.

Beltane is the time for loving and life
    as a horn begins the chase,
The Maiden seeks her lover and friend
    for the Goddess to embrace.

Lugnasadh's sun beats hard and hot
    on fields ripe with Her gift,
Cornucopia's belly is ours to enjoy
    while summer spirits lift.

Samhain brings forth the mysterious dark
    when spirits walk the night,
The forces are strong and powerful
    as autumn takes its flight.

8

Childlike

ne of the best aspects of the Craft is the open-mindedness with which we can practice our faith, do our work, and raise our children. We have no problem with other religions or philosophies. Indeed, we welcome them into our learning, for they present us with a clearer and wider view of our world and the brothers and sisters in it.

We tend to raise our children to learn about and know other religions and beliefs. We live the Craft, so we have firm foundations in it. We want our children to make their own choices about religious paths when they are old enough to do so. But for this to be an opportunity for them, we must ensure that they are well versed in many belief systems so that they may make an informed choice. I have only met one or two witches who were absolutely determined that their children would practice the Craft, come hell or high water. But I find this to be a most unfortunate attitude. Children eventually become adults. It is up to us to ensure that they have the tools and knowledge to become informed and open-minded adults. If we, ourselves, are closed to other possibilities in life, so will our children be closed. For their sake, we must teach them what we can of the world in which they must live. They must know the different cultures, religions, and races of this planet. Yes, we are all brothers and sisters, but the differences in our peoples are what makes us unique and interesting.

Each time we teach our children about a new thing, we open the road to their futures. But, by keeping them from learning or experiencing new ideas and beliefs, we are sheltering them from the reality of their world. Closed-mindedness is akin to racism, prejudice, and bigotry. These things are not to be tolerated in a Wiccan home. They are against the nature of our faith and beliefs. So we give our children all the knowledge that they can absorb. And we hope that someday they will find the peace and self-discovery which our faith gives us.

This open-mindedness is precisely why the Wiccaning Ceremony for a child is one of giving the child over to knowledge. We vow to do nothing which will stand in the way of a child's right to grow and learn. The babe must be presented with choices and then given the support he or she needs while making life's decisions. We use the ceremony as a "stepping off" place from which all paths lead.

For you Wiccan parents who wish to have "craft times" with your children, we will discuss ritual, games, personal child altars, sleepy-time herbs to use, and a child's interpretation of the Charge of the Goddess.

Take the time with your children to show them the gentle and comforting practices of our faith. Do with them the spells which will give them self-confidence and ability. Play with them the psychic games offered here. Childhood abilities are often more powerful and more finely tuned than our own. What they feel and see about them can be most interesting. Their perceptions of the world around them often include those unseen places which adulthood tends to fade.

But most importantly, be with your children! The greatest and most magical gift you can give your children is to give of your time and yourself. They will treasure these moments, and the memories they will have will become part of the source for their magical pursuits later. For love *is* the source of magic. Love is the place from which all compassion, power, and positive energy flows. All things we do, rituals we dance, and homes we care for begin and end with love.

Rituals

Rituals for children are quite different from adult rituals. For children, the big picture presents too esoteric a view of their world. They must break this world down into components of the whole. Color, texture, smell, and shape are all things that children can relate to. They take these pieces of the universe and examine them. They are then equipped to bring them together to create a whole picture. For young children, the intangible can be extremely difficult to describe. They may experience or feel things, but may not know how to communicate these feelings.

Begin crafting with your children when they begin to question you about your magical tools and practices. If they are curious, then it is time to give them things to contemplate. But for their sake and yours, *don't build them clocks*. They only asked "the time," not the creative engineering of the clock's mechanism. They will ask questions about that later if they are interested. But for now, they just want simple questions answered simply.

One aspect of the Craft which can be taught and reinforced from an early age is respect for craft items and work-in-progress. If your children ask you "what that stuff is doing" on the mantle, answer gently and tell them that those items are there "answering mommy/daddy's prayers." They may, of course, launch the barrage of questions that fill their little heads, or they may be quite satisfied with the simple answer you give and question further later. Either way, this kind of answer is an honest, gentle stepping stone to a myriad of discussions.

If your children question your ritual practices *in comparison* with a friend's parents, you have a perfect opportunity to find out what those practices may be and educate your children in the lessons of difference. Take each questioning time in your childrens lives as an opportunity to open their eyes to our world. Consider each as a chance to grow, yourself.

Children love to dance and sing. They love movement. Lofting a scarf, chanting a chant, singing the Charge or dancing in circles are all activities that parents and children can do together. And children *love* repetition. Over and over and over again. They chant rhymes and words and sounds. They sing songs so many times that you end up hearing it in your head for the rest of the day. They love repeating themselves. So take advantage of this and teach them poetry, songs, and dances of the old ways. Listen to Celtic harp music and relaxation tapes with gentle waves and instrumentals. Or teach them ring dances and celebrational chants. Invent these things together. Children are wonderfully creative and they rarely hold back. When they have an idea, listen. And develop your simple ritual techniques together. You will continue to add more complex material to your childrens appetite for knowledge as it grows.

Safe non-toxic herbs are a wonderful tool to help children understand the value of growing things and what can be done with them. Herbs such as thyme, basil, and mint have soothing qualities and sweet scents. Teach them to notice differences in scent, texture, color, etc. Help them tune into the energy of the plants. Have them hold and touch them. Let them make pictures from them with glue and paper. The point is to generate interest in the many facets and tools of our faith. As their interest grows, they will let you know. They will ask you questions. Sometimes incessantly!

Once your children have expressed interest in a particular facet of the Craft, bring it into your simplified rituals. The herbs that they now feel comfortable with can be used for enjoyment and participation in the ritual. Teach them the power of the herbs and let them decide how to use them. They will come up with something, I assure you. Correct them if they get off on a tangent which strays from the basic meanings, but otherwise, children will enjoy having some control over a few parts of the ritual.

Crystals are something small children can begin to collect for their very own crystal garden. Instead of silica sand, use soft folds of cloth or mounds of quilt batting. Let them collect the smoother ones for a time until they are ready for the more delicate ones. Show children how to enhance a garden with their own personal treasures. Arrangement and rearrangement will interest them more than a garden that they are not allowed to touch.

Children love "treasure boxes." Help them craft a "magical box." Use an old shoe box or other appropriate container. Let them decorate it and style it to their own taste. Make it a rainy-day project. And have them collect treasures and magical finds in that container.

A Child's Personal Altar/Hearth

Many Wiccan parents start their children off with a few basics, like a wand that is just the right size. Let them find a wand on one of your walks. They'll know if it feels comfortable. Many of the things children collect or will use are often considered a game. But this is natural and they will develop a more serious approach later. The Goddess loves the laughter of children, so let them have fun with the Craft.

A child's altar can begin with something as simple as a willow wand. Add to that a pretty jar of dried or fresh herbs or flowers. Stones, shells, and feathers will find their way to your little one's magical place. A bowl or some pouches you have made together make perfect holders for "collected works."

Allow children to use items that you feel are safe and interesting. Discuss the elements in a way that children could understand.

Psychic Games

Children are receptive to just about any game. They love to play and will try new things. The following are two games to play with children which will help develop their abilities of sensory perception.

Sand Visions

For this, you will need a shallow, wide bowl of sand and a popsicle stick or pencil. Explain that you want the children to close their eyes and see if something pops into their heads. Tell them to draw what they see in the sand. You can begin to insert more specific requests as time goes on, but the idea behind this is to see if they are empathic to the environment and to your own thought patterns. You can also switch roles and they can try to transmit their mind's pictures to you. You then draw what you perceive in the sand. It is an exercise you will all benefit from over time.

Hot and Cold

All of us have played this at one time or another. You remember, you pick an object in the room and then direct the seeker by calling out "hot," or "cold," depending on how close or far the person is from the object. Children think this game is great because they feel that you are not really "telling" them where to go to find the object and they perceive themselves as having some control over where they are seeking.

In this version, tell your children to listen to their little voice and go to or away from the area they think the object is in. You will guide them if they go too far astray. Tell them to go slowly and you will "think" hot or cold. They will try to tune into your feelings and will develop abilities to perceive subtle changes to your body language, breathing, and thought energy patterns. They will become more astute with practice and may want to switch places with you eventually, although children usually like to be on the seeking end of games like this.

Sleepy Time Pillows

Sleepy time pillows are really very simple to make and use. Because children have a tendency toward mild reactions to grain dust and weeds, this pillow is not recommended for use in bed. Children's faces should not go near it as the herbal mixture inside does let off a certain amount of dust.

Choose any picture or shape you would like your pillow to resemble. Make it approximately six-to-eight-inches square. Cut the shape out twice and sew the pillow together on the backside of the fabric (you will be turning it inside out) keeping the good sides together, facing each other in the middle. Leave an opening approximately three inches in length.

In a bowl, mix 1 part valerian, 2 parts camomile flowers, and 1 part lavender. All of these are generally available at any health food store. You should end up with a mixture no larger than 1 cupful. Add to that 2 cups of foam chips and mix this really well. Turn your pillow right side out and stuff it with this mixture. Sew up the opening and add bows, buttons, or other appealing decoration. The pillow will sit on a shelf and each night before bed, your children can give it a little shake to release it's sleepy-time properties. Each of these herbs has the most wonderful relaxation qualities, and your children will develop faith in the pillow's power.

A Child's Charge of the Goddess

The Charge of the Goddess is a powerful story told in first person by a High Priestess when she feels the Goddess within her during ritual. She has become empowered with the authority and right to speak the words of her Lady.

But because of it's ancient tone, the Charge is not understood by children. They may listen and hear what is being said, but understanding or comprehension of the meaning is not really within their grasp, somewhat like trying Shakespeare on them. So the following is a version of the Charge I wrote a long time ago to make it understandable for children.

The Charge

These are the words of the Goddess:

"If you are in need, gather with your family when the Moon is full. And you will know that you are with those who love you as I do. I am the spirit of all that is Craft.

"There, in that place, you will learn our ways but not all of our greatest wisdom. You will learn as you grow with your family in love.

"You will dance and sing, celebrate, and feast for me. What I am is the joy which you feel when you gather like this. I am glad when I see you happy with those you love because I am Love, love for all living things.

"Keep your thoughts on what is good; keep working to learn more about your world. Do not let anyone tell you that your hopes and dreams are not right. The path of good, my path, will take you to a place where all of the lessons will be understood.

"I give you joy, but you must use it. It is my gift, and it will bring you happiness. While you are alive, I give you knowledge about your spirit, and tell you that your body may die, but you, your spirit, lives on and on. And after you die, I will make sure you are peaceful and free, and will see those you love once more.

"I ask nothing from you. I give you these gifts with no expectations. You must decide to take the path of love and goodness on your own. That is what you must do with my gifts. I give you my love regardless.

"You see me in the green of the Earth and in the white glow of the Moon. I am the tides and oceans, and I wait for you to join me.

"When you are doing something because of love, you see me in your heart. So, feel love and beauty, feel strong but be kind, do the right thing, but do not boast.

"If you look for me, you will not find me, unless you know the answer to the Mystery of Life. If you know that answer, then you know you must look for me inside yourself. I live in your heart, not apart from you. You are the one to call on my strength when you need me. I will be there.

"For I was with you from the beginning and I will be with you forever."

So speaks the Goddess.

9

Cat Magic

nimals are as much a part of the Goddess as are people. They express themselves in a different manner but do not let their differences fool you. Animals are powerful and wise. Each type of living thing has its own particular form of communication and wisdom. Nothing that is alive is without an intellect of some kind. From one-celled micro-organisms, to plants, to animals, to people, having life means the presence of a functioning intelligence. We must respect the life of things around us as we respect human life. I believe in animal preservation but at the same time, I see the need for species reduction, as in the example of Humane Societies and their policy on mandatory sterilization of adopted pets.

Pets are there to co-exist with us. They are not there to be abused, ignored, or mistreated in any way. If you are the type of person who cannot put an animal's needs somewhere on your priority list, then perhaps you should buy a pet rock. I hear they are very forgiving. If, on the other hand, you love animals as I do, you respect their needs and care for your friends as you do anything else that you love.

Animals and their human partners have a most unique bond. It is like no human bonding we know. There simply is no comparison. My animals and I have always had special relationships. I have never become a pet "owner" by any other circumstance but pure fate. Each of my pets has been a gift from Her. They sought me out, not the other way around. My acquisition of them came to pass by some kind of mystical weave in the fabric of my life. I have had many beloved friends and I miss each of them as they passed out of my life. There have been cats and dogs, hamsters, and birds. I got to know each one and learned lessons from each one. However small or insignificant they seemed at the time, these lessons have stayed with me.

For my taste, cats are a prime pets for witches. Hokey as that may seem to the non-Wiccan reader, considering the stereotypical picture of a witch with her ever-present black cat, cats have personalities that compliment a person of the Craft. They are independent, need little supervision or care aside from filling bowls and changing the litter. They don't require walks and they don't desire to please their owner. No, cats tend to curl their lip at your attempts to reprimand or induce them to a certain behavior. They prefer the perverse approach to your scolding. But when you have work to do or, are otherwise occupied, you can bet they'll choose that moment to want attention.

But the very trait that makes cats annoying (independence) is the exact trait we witches must have to practice our faith. When we become too dependent on something outside ourselves, we have a tendency to set our magical pursuits further and further to the side. We let go. For a time. But to practice in a total and free way, we must know that we are the masters of our own destiny, we are the creators of our own script, and we are in control of our goals and pursuits. That is why we can relate to feline mentality. They practice what we strive to achieve.

Their annoying habits aside, cats are wonderful magic-mates. They know when we are working, and quietly lend a power boost to our efforts. They see all that is happening around them, so they act as a barometer, and enable us to gage our concentrated power by their reactions. They help to do these things when you need them the most, too. When you are lacking energy and must do work, they are there for you. Cats sense their partner's moods and energy levels. They even know to occupy your lap for stroking if you really need a lift. Mind you, they do have a hidden agenda for that one, but we need them, too.

When cats are in a playful mood, just about anything will entertain them. Make a pouch from any fabric you have around the house and stuff it with catnip or valerian root. They will love you forever. Catnip acts on a cat's chemical structure. You heard me right, folks. Catnip gives them a high. They scratch, roll, and dive into it if you spread a little of the crushed leaves on the floor. But watch the smell on your skin. It is not one of the most pleasant. It is an easy plant to grow indoors and before you know it, you'll have bundles hung to dry. Catnip is as perverse as it's feline namesake, and will grow despite just about anything you can do to it. But keep it in a hanging basket if you grow it indoors. Your four-legged friend will attempt to use the plant before you clip it, so beware.

Cats have their own peculiar form of magic. It is truly no small wonder that history has placed them in unique focus. In the greatest days of Egypt's dynasties, cats were revered as an earthly representative of one of their gods. During the Dark and Middle Ages, cats were allowed to procreate to their little hearts content to help keep rat populations down. Rats carried plagues and cats killed rats, so their usefulness became associated not with help, but with disease. They became the favorite companion of herb women and gained the reputation of being a witch's familiar. A familiar is a non-human "helper" of magical pursuits. Herb women were knowledgable about the plants and remedies available in their area. They were not evil, nor did they go about cursing the townfolk. Rather, herb women became a threat to the male-dominated Church at the approaching peak of its control. Not only did these healing women threaten the practices of male-only doctoring, but they threatened the very foundations of the Church and all it stood for. Herb women were, in general, midwives.

Women, according to Church teachings, were to don the cloak of pain in penance for Original Sin. We suffered labor and tearing for the sake of humankind. The painful process of labor was ours to keep for tempting Adam in the Garden of Eden. With Church-condoned midwives at their bedsides, women were given no relief from the pain of birthing because herbal remedies and concoctions were the "Devil's work." They were not for sinful humans.

Over the course of time, herbal women were condemned as witches and Europe went crazy. Witch trials were popular and none could speak out for they, too, would be tortured, burned, or hanged. No one was safe from the tyranny. One needed only to cast aspersions on one's neighbor to cause suspicion. The insanity continued as the religious fervor peaked and thousands upon thousands of innocent people were killed.

Cats were burned with their mistresses. If they could be found, that is. They were not easily captured and their reputation as sly, evil creatures grew. But history tells a slanted story. Herb women/midwives knew how to ease the labor and pain of childbirth. They knew what teas cured fever; they knew the poultice that banished infection. Their knowledge was vast and their desire to heal gave them power that only the pure of intent can achieve. The cats were given a very bad reputation and were guilty by association.

Cats are indeed, helpers of magic. They will aid their true master or mistress in his or her pursuit of the magical secrets. They appear and disappear at will. (Reread that sentence over and over and it will still say the same thing!) I believe that cats have a unique ability to "wink-out." Remember the Cheshire Cat with his lingering grin? Well, why not. Cats can be "all of a sudden" there and "all of a sudden" gone. How do you explain it? Too often, I have seen my cats be at my side and then gone, never having seen them enter or leave. No noise, no meow, no movement, nothing. They just seem to be able to wink in and out. But that is part of their charm and magic.

If you really take the time to get to know your animal's personality, likes and dislikes, your bond could go on forever. He does not belong to you. On the contrary, according to your feline friend, you belong to him! So lavish him with love and he will remain your steadfast companion. Invite him into your circle. Many cats prefer the position of watcher from the outside perimeter, but like to be invited nonetheless. They will lend support at the time you raise the power. Their eyes never leave you and they tense with anticipation of that power's release to its goal. Watch your cat as you work the Craft. You will see recognition and the desire to "be involved."

IN CONCLUSION

Gentle Reader,

I have enjoyed sharing these words with you. This book is peppered with bits and pieces of magical knowledge I have gathered over the years. My work comes from a combination of learning from others and my own intuition and imagination. I have said it repeatedly, but here it is once again:

TRUST IN YOURSELF!

If you do not trust yourself, you do not recognize the power of the Gods. You ignore the love of the Goddess. For you and She are one. You must trust that you will recognize what is comfortable and what is not. She will not misguide you if you put your faith in yourself. Look for the power deep in your heart. If you seek the Mysteries with pure intention, you will find what you seek.

Be creative. She gave us an imagination to use, not to stagnate! Let it flow freely. You will find that your power increases and magic becomes a delightful part of your life. Let it call to you from different corners of your home. Build places for your heart's work. Surround yourself with magical things. Enjoy what daily magic has to offer.

Be aware. Awareness will give you the answers. They are there for you to see if you will open your eyes. When you ask for help, or you are in emotional need, those prayers are answered. But often, if you are involved in yourself and your feelings, your eyes are not seeing clearly. Look for the signs. She provides them but it is up to you to make use of them. Take note of the times when your needs were met by "coincidence." These answers did not just "happen." They were presented to you. You only had to notice they were there.

For the novice witch, examination is the paramount ingredient for magical work. You MUST examine your motives and goals. If any part of your examination yields a negative response, stop. Take a second look and see where you are straying. Your work must harm no one and that includes yourself. Vengeful acts and curses are for the weak of spirit. The Lady will fill you with light, you just have to ask.

The life of a witch is one of peace and contentment, knowing that She will guide us on our path. Grow and learn. Yes, life hands us some hard knocks at times. But with love and faith in our hearts, we muddle through. And we ALWAYS come out a better person for having experienced it. That may not always seem the case, but the lessons we learn, regardless of their focus, were needed ones.

The greatest magic you can practice is that of loving. Be with your loved ones and friends. Take time to enjoy them. Our lives are but a brief stop on the journey. Take advantage of the time you have together. Love your home. Make it a place to shed the outside world from your shoulders. Enrich your life with love and you will know the true meaning of Magic.

Goddess Bless!

Appendix 1
Home for the Modern Pagan

The world is an enormously busy place. When we leave our homes, we enter a dimension that can be very stressful. Negative and positive energies rush at us from all directions. My home is my safe place and when I come through the door, I immediately start to shed all the wound-up energy that I bring home. I begin to relax and let my senses fill with all that is "me" in my little corner of this world. Add to that my family and I become a whole person again.

The reasons for the subtitle of this book must be obvious by now. More than anything, those who practice earth religions *must* have a place to ground and become one with their world again. I have gone through blocks of time where my home got away from me. A particularly painful breakup left me with an empty home. Oh, I had furniture and belongings (including magical tools) but my home was not a home. It was a house. A place. None of me was there. I had not done any indoor or outdoor gardening, no magical work, and very little laughing. It just didn't feel like home. Even friends commented on its lack of energy. It was an unusual time for me. Over time, I pulled myself together. As I struggled to become emotionally healthy again, my home began to bloom. With each step toward the Self, my home went through a transition, too.

We cannot alter the fact that our homes are part of our Self. Nor would we want to. That is not to say that it has to be a particular place. Many people make a home wherever they are living at the time. Home is an attitude. With the right attitude, you can become one with your place. And as a witch, I am compelled by my deepest faith to take every opportunity to touch the Mother and Father. To feel the cool earth and to revel in the golden heat of the sun.

All that is nature and beauty and love is there for the asking, whether we live in the city or the country. We can garden, decorate, cook, and magically bring Her into our home to enhance and energize this most important place.

The following pages contain some of my favorite recipes. They are divided into three categories. First is magical cooking, then medicinal remedies, and finally, recipes for sure-fire magical solutions to everyday problems. I hope that these add to whatever store of knowledge you are building and that they work as well for you as they have for me. Some are handed down from women of my line, some are modified from recipes collected through friends, and some are recipes I have developed on my own over time and many trials. As is the tradition of our truly free religion, use them with my love. Stay joyful in your work and you will have added the most important ingredient to any recipe. The deepest mysteries shall open to those who find joy and love in their magical and mundane pursuits.

Basic Recipes

Any recipe named for a particular sabbat (or moon phase or element) can be used at any time. The ingredients are particularly potent at the celebration for which it has been named, but its power does not decrease when used at other times.

Full Moon Mulled Wine

Equal parts cranberry juice
            apple juice
            pear juice
to about 3 quarts.

Bring juices to a slow simmer in a non-metal pot.
Add: 7 whole cloves
     the grated peel of 1 orange
     the grated peel of 1 lemon

Let this simmer about one hour. For the final five minutes of simmer, add one quart of medium to dry white wine.

Serve hot or warm with a twist of lemon and a small pinch of cinnamon or a stick.

Sabbat Sage Bread

This bread is used at sabbats for the wisdom required to celebrate the true aspects of a given holiday. Our sabbats are a time of celebration. As a witch preferring to work solo, I use the sabbats as a time for renewal, learning, magic, and celebration. Sage is a deep enhancement for learning. Use it with good intent and your sabbats will become more focused. Begin with any bread recipe with which you feel comfortable. This can include any whole grain or gluten-free recipes you may prefer. At the end of your last rising and just before you put them in the oven, set your loaves aside and mix together the following per loaf:

3 tsp. chopped chives or green onion tips (these can be frozen
    ahead without much loss of flavor)
1/2 tsp. sage
1/4 tsp. dill
1/2 tsp. garlic (optional)
2 level tsp. butter

Grind and mash the herbs into the soft butter and add:

1-1/2 tsp. plain low fat yogurt

Brush this mixture on top of your loaves and slit the bread length-wise to brush into the cut. Bake as normal and serve hot if possible.

Pasta Sauce for Lovers

Add to your favorite pasta sauce recipe:

basil, rosemary and celery seed to taste.

Before taking the dish to the table, pour the sauce over your cooked pasta, lay paper thin slices of cheese over top in a casserole dish and sprinkle liberally with basil as you spell for love. Place under the broiler for about 2 minutes and you have a dish that is not only potent but powerful!

Samhain Squash Soup

This soup is ideal for the time around Samhain because of its main ingredient. Squash is a fall vegetable harvested just before Samhain. The wonderful yellows and oranges of the common varieties blends well with the eerie and firelike aspects of Samhain.

Begin with two large squash, cleaned and cubed.

Boil in plenty of water until just tender. Do not drain.

Into the pot add:

3 chopped onions
1/2 cup barley
carrots if desired
3 or 4 celery stalks, chopped
1/2 loaf stale bread, cubed (this acts as a thickener)

Suggested seasonings include sage, thyme, dill and rosemary

Slow simmer for about an hour or until barley is tender, stirring often. About ten minutes before serving, stir in about 1/2 cup of sour cream (low fat of course!) and stir until smooth. Serve with warm herb breads or muffins and enjoy the bounty of the season. It is healthy, vegetarian and low, low fat.

The above soup can also be made with a base of cubed beets instead of squash. If you are using beets, eliminate the rosemary; the two tastes do not compliment each other.

Summer Vegetable Casserole

5 stalks celery, chopped
1 lb. mushrooms, washed and halved
1 clove garlic, mashed
large bunch broccoli, tops only (save stalks for soup)
1/2 head cauliflower, chopped

In a small amount of butter, soften celery and garlic over low heat. Add touches of water if needed to avoid burning. Steam other veggies to tender. In a casserole dish, mix steamed vegetables and the celery mixture. Add one can of any vegetable creamed soup in its concentrate form.

Mix well. Fold in 1 beaten egg, parmesan cheese and 1/4 cup low fat yogurt. Flatten top of mix and sprinkle liberally with bread crumbs. Dot with butter or margarine and bake about 45 minutes at 350 degrees.

Medicinal Remedies

Like any other health solutions, medicinal use of herbs should be studied and carefully considered before use. Don't take any one person's word on a particular plant. Consult as many herbals as you can and be cautious of allergic-positive plants. If, for example, you have an allergy to fungus or mould, plants from this category would obviously not be for you.

As with anything you put in your body, do it with magic in mind. Use the full potential of any plant that you wish to try. The following are just a few basic simples that will help to relieve everyday ailments.

Stress Headaches

Use Camomile tea for tension and stress headaches. Brew a tea-spoon of the dried herb in 1 cup boiling water. Cover while steeping to hold the steam. Steep about 2 minutes. Find a quiet place to sip your tea and relax.

Bad Breath

Chew fresh parsley for halitosis. If this is unavailable, brew a mild cup of parsley tea and sip, holding the tea in your mouth for a moment.

Fever

For mild fevers related to infection, sun stroke, etc., brew a cup of dandelion tea. Dandelion can be purchased at most health food stores and is high in iron.

Nausea

For mild nausea due to flue or food reactions, try tea made from basil or peppermint. Check with your doctor before use if you are pregnant and suffering morning sickness.

Nervousness

For bouts of nervousness due to upcoming events or stress, a mild tea of rosemary will calm you. Take care to use only about 1/2 teaspoon per cup of water as rosemary can cause flatulence. This could result in embarrassment!

Congestion

Thyme tea cannot be beat for relieving congestion due to colds. Use also as a steam. Boil the water and throw in the thyme. Breathe in the steam while covering your head with a towel.

Magical Solutions

Throughout this book, I have given you ways to use magic in your home. Spelling is an individual thing, able to be modified for the practitioner and the goal. But certain herbs are particularly strong for one or two goals in spellwork. Try these, and you'll see results within one cycle of the moon. Remember, spells don't always work just as you expect. Prayer can be answered in many ways. Keep your eyes open and you will see the solutions come to you.

For needed income:
Burn pinches of dill on your coal throughout the full moon cycle for immediate answers regarding needed money or work opportunities.

For love to come your way, or to strengthen existing bonds:
Boil basil and orange peel in a small pot during the waxing moon (growth phase).

Healing for yourself or another:
Rowan is difficult to obtain most of the time but would be the best to use. You can also try hawthorn. Take 3 leaves, wrap in a soft piece of purple or blue felt and tie with a thread. Tuck into a dark place for the duration of the dark of the moon.

To rid your house of an unwanted guest:
This spell is, of course, done without malice. Use a yarrow stem to bundle with your intention written on a small piece of paper. Place at the exit to your home and guests will wish to leave on their own.

To enhance business dealings:
Carry a small packet of dandelion with you to meetings and contract signings. The translation from the French word is "tooth of the lion" and it gives you the courage you need to negotiate a decent and fair deal.

To enhance psychic abilities:
Crush sage leaves between your hands and inhale the wonderfully earthy aroma. Gently rub the scent into the area of your temples and breathe deeply. Practice your work as usual.

To bring peace to your home:
Burn plenty of jasmine. This is usually obtained in the form of incense. Try to get as pure a form as you can. Scent all areas of your home, including corners. Bury jasmine sticks at each corner of your house outside to protect and bring peace.

Appendix 2
Color Guide*

The elements each have a color which is representative of that particular realm. These should be used, or at the very least, kept in mind, whenever you are working with the elements themselves. They are helpful in visualization as you call up the Quarter Guards, as well. They are: red (fire), yellow (earth), blue (air) and green (water). They may not seem to physically correspond to the actual properties of the elements (blue theoretically should be used for water), but the appearance of discrepancy is understood of learned witches. The following list should prove helpful.

Black: corresponds to the Cabala at Binah (or Compassion) and shows dominion over the underworld. It is a color that absorbs all others, and many witches have extensive wardrobes of black. I find that to wear black when I am doing a psychic reading is helpful.

Blue: corresponds to the Cabala at Chesed (or Mercy). It is a color often used when trying to sort out emotional difficulties, such as impatience, anger, and jealousy.

Red: corresponds to the Cabala Geburah (or Strength). This is a color of force. Not a negative force but rather the kind of force used to fight psychic attack. Red is a color worn by many witches in the Mother stage of their lives. It is a color representing the blood of birth and is therefore full of the lifegiving fluids. Many witches will wear their red cords as a belt for a robe.

Green: corresponds to the Cabala Netzach (or Victory). This is a color rich in accomplishment and success. Mint green is a particularly good color for a success-oriented work. It is also the color most witches associate with spells for prosperity.

Originally published in *Of Witches*, by Janet Thompson (York Beach, ME: Samuel Weiser, 1993), p. 54. Reprinted here for your convenience.

Yellow: corresponds to the Cabala Tiphareth (or Beauty). It is a color which gives off a tremendous vibration and should be worm when feeling low or tired.

Reddish-brown: corresponds to the Cabala Malkuth (or the Lower Kingdom). This, of course, does not imply the underworld, but rather the physical world that surrounds us. When needing to be your most alert in the mundane world, this is the color used.

Gold and **Silver:** have had some argument from different traditions. The two are both colors that correspond to the Cabala Kether (or the Godhead). They are represented in Wicca as the Sun and Moon. Often, a male witch will wear gold for the God aspect and a female witch will wear silver for the Goddess aspect. I wear both. I have come to terms with my animus and I feel very comfortable representing both God and Goddess in my personal tastes. Silver and gold have long been considered sacred colors and they continue to be so. Their value on the world market shows their value in the physical world, as well. They are beautiful in the light of the candles in Circle and they let off the most spectacular emanations.

This is a general outline of the basic colors we deal with. Most witches have a cord of each for spell work. Color learning is greatly dependent on the intuitive powers of the witch and the traits of the various colors must be experienced to be understood. By this I mean that the colors must be used to be known. It is as simple as that. A novice can be handed a certain color cord, but without direction, that witch will not grasp the deep relation between the color of the cord and its use.

Index

A practicing witch since childhood, Janet Thompson has been a Wiccan High Priestess for over a decade. She holds a B.A. in classical and medieval folklore with a minor in philosophy from the University of Windsor. A certified Master Herbalist consultant who lives in Canada, Thompson is the author of the popular *Of Witches: Celebrating the Goddess as a Solitary Pagan*, also published by Weiser.